THE
BATTLE FOR

THE
BOOK

COVER PHOTOGRAPH
St. Catherine's Monastery, Sinai, Israel.
DAVID CURRIE
BACK COVER PHOTOGRAPHS
(Top) Papyrus fragment from the Gospel of Mark, third century.
(Bottom) The Shrine of the Book (contains Dead Sea Scrolls), Jerusalem
DAVID MARSHALL
(Inset) The Ishtar Gate, Babylon, Iraq.
DAVID CURRIE

First published 1991

Printed and published by
The Stanborough Press Limited for
Autumn House Publications
Alma Park, Grantham, NG31 9SL, England

ISBN 0-904748-58-8

THE BATTLE FOR THE BOOK

by DAVID MARSHALL Ph.D.

The story of how the Bible was written, who wrote it, and when.

The story of how the sixty-six books of the Bible came to be regarded as special and were brought together.

The story of how the Bible survived the centuries and how battle after battle was fought over its accuracy and (under remarkable circumstances) won.

The story of how astonishing manuscript and archaeological finds have, time after time, proved the Bible right and its critics wrong.

The story of the English Bible through Caedmon of Whitby, King Alfred the Great, John Wyclif, William Tyndale, J. B. Phillips — to the Revised English Bible.

ANCIENT MIDDLE EAST

BLACK SEA

ARMENIA

CASPIAN
SEA

Carchemish

Harran

Antioch

Shamra
(garit)

Nineveh
Nimrud

PERSIA (IRAN)

River Euphrates

Palmyra

River Tigris

Behistun

Baalbek

MESOPOTAMIA
(IRAQ)

Damascus

NE
o

Babylon
Kish

Susa

JORDAN

Ur

PERSIAN
GULF

ARABIA

CONTENTS

The author wishes to express his profound thanks to archaeologist Dr. William Shea for ensuring the accuracy of Section Four and that the narrative incorporated the most up-to-date findings.

Introduction

A controversial book

This book has always been a hot commodity.

People have been gaoled for reading it.

Men have been burned for translating it.

Others have been transported for spreading its teachings.

It has been banned and burned in countries scared of its influence. It has been described as 'the most subversive single volume in existence'. In the years before *glasnost* a secret network existed to smuggle it under the Iron Curtain. Smugglers caught distributing it disappeared without trace.

The man who first began to translate it into English was hounded by the government for most of his life. Some years after his death his body was exhumed and his remains burned.

The next man to attempt an English translation was forced to flee the country. In Germany, as he proceeded with his task, he was shadowed by undercover agents working for three different governments. With the project near to completion the authorities moved in, broke up the type and came within a hair's breadth of capturing him. He escaped in a boat along the Rhine under cover of darkness.

A few years later he was arrested in the Netherlands, strangled and burned.

It has been lampooned, ridiculed, denounced, vilified and shot down in flames as no other book has. The critics have attacked its factual accuracy; the characters and nations whose activities it records have been laughed off as 'mythical'. But under the fierce glare of scientific enquiry and archaeological research its assertions have been authenticated as fact. Time and time again its critics have been forced to withdraw in disarray.

The book was right. The critics were wrong.

But the critics then simply shifted their ground and began to shoot from another angle.

Meanwhile the scholars worked on. The archaeologists continued their digging. Tablets inscribed with ancient cuneiform writing came to light, artifacts were uncovered. And the assertions made so dogmatically by another school of 'experts' were proved groundless. The *tells*, the ancient cities and settlements of the Middle East, seem to be replete with layer upon layer of artifacts waiting to provide mute though eloquent testimony to the book's detailed accuracy.

Those artifacts, the magnificent stone walls, the archways still imposing though ravaged by the aeons, those tablets and parchments — in conference and through the tools of modern science and the analysis of sharp minds — have at so many points verified the book that nerves tingle and those with an open mind are obliged to entertain at least the possibility that behind the book stands the divine presence.

Portions of this book have been translated into more than 1,710 languages. In a single year fifty million copies were produced in the United States alone. The *Business Monitor* tells us that each year, an average of £4.1 million is spent in *Britain* on copies of this book. It also tells us that £6.3 million worth are exported from Britain each year. A spokesman for an organization that promotes its sale reports that all that amounts to a grand total of over 3,466,000 copies per annum.

But statistics are misleading; and never more so than in this instance. If this ancient book is a best seller, it is not a best seller in the sense that the paperbacks of Jackie Collins, Frederick Forsyth and Harold Robbins are best sellers. *In fact, it is probably the world's least read best seller.*

But, for all that, there is a strange, unaccountable fascination about it.

And why?

Is it viewed as a talisman, a good luck charm?

Or is there a feeling — albeit a vague one — that between its covers lies a wisdom that discerns the end from the beginning, and lends meaning to the journey from cradle to grave; a window on origin and destiny, time and eternity?

Is there a feeling — ah yes, irrational, even 'superstitious' — that the great Power behind the universe inspired the minds and experience of the forty men who wrote this book that has proved so durable? And that, if that is the case, it may, just *may*, have something to say to *us*?

Has there been a reaction to the feeling that success in life is entirely to be measured by the acquisition of material possessions? To the assumption that ultimate truth emerges only from scientific laboratories? To the idea that trying to make sense of so complex and sophisticated a world is simply too much to ask?

A reaction, perhaps to the unthinking acceptance that the kind of 'sense' made of things by Sigmund Freud, Charles Darwin and Karl Marx is not the last word, that their 'received wisdom' poses more questions than it answers?

Or am I going too far, too fast? Raising blood pressure, overheating collars?

The voices of even the most 'rational' of people become shrill, and their persons embarrassed and uncomfortable when the suggestion is made that such an ancient book might have something to say in the age of computers and silicon chips. Preposterous. A fall-back to an age of superstition best forgotten. Yes?

Perhaps our world is so problem free that we are no longer in need of super-human guidance delivered through some inspired book. . . . Or perhaps life really *is* what our present-day 'wise men' tell us it is — 'a nightmare between two eternities', 'the penalty for the crime of being born', a 'dusty scuffle over a parched terrain'. . . . Perhaps the human race really *is* no more than 'a planetary eczema' with each member merely 'an enlarged protein molecule, potential fertilizer'. . . .

So many times this book — and, therefore its explanation of the meaning of life — has been 'debunked'. And then, as if stubbornly unwilling to quit, has made a comeback.

In the Age of Reason, Voltaire gave a lecture on it in his Paris home. He said the old book was, without question, completely obsolete and that, within a century of that date, would be out of print, unobtainable. That was in the eighteenth century. One century on from the year in which Voltaire gave his lecture the home in which he had given it was a centre dedicated to the distribution of the book he had written off as obsolete. His words were forgotten, but his home was used to distribute this book in scores of languages to the furthest reaches of the globe. Voltaire had made an unquestionable contribution to the thought and life of his age; but is it possible that the book he declared obsolete is ageless — relevant in every age?

The book, of course, is the Bible, for Christians the Book of books.

Could this ancient book that won't quit be worth a second look? Does it really have something to say to our modern age? Is it worth while to take a second glance at the evidence unearthed in recent years for its accuracy and authenticity?

In a society like ours, in a world like ours — isn't *anything* worth a try?

SECTION ONE

WHERE THE BIBLE CAME FROM

1

How the Bible was written

Paul, who wrote about two thirds of the part of the Bible called the New Testament, fell foul of the Roman Empire. During the last winter of his life, under sentence of death, he smuggled a letter to his student Timothy. In it we find these words:

'Do your best to come to me quickly. . . . When you come, bring the cloak that I left with Carpus at Troas, and my scrolls, especially the parchments.' [1]

He wanted his heavy overcoat. How could a scholar concentrate on his studies in a dank, draughty, below-ground-level Roman dungeon?

To have his scrolls and parchments to hand was even more vital.

Following the conquests of Alexander the Great after 336BC the world had been Hellenized. Everyone who was anyone spoke the *Koine*, the Greek dialect common to all countries. Paul was no exception. Hence the word he used for cloak was *phailones*, the word for scrolls was *biblion*, and the word for parchments, *membrana*.

The Greek words for scrolls and parchments reflected the material from which they were made.

A *biblion* was a reed-plant which grew on river banks or in marshy conditions. The inner leaf or bark of this plant was dried in strips, and rows of the dried strips — crisscross fashion — were gummed together to make a writing material.

The Greek word *membrana* was actually borrowed from Latin and means 'membrane'. This was part of an animal skin also processed for use as a writing material.

But in tracing the origin of the word Bible, *biblion* is the clue. Among the alternative names for the plant from which it was made was *byblos*. This name was given by the Greeks to a town in Phoenicia: Byblos.

When referring to the Old and New Testaments, Greek-speaking Christians use the words *ta biblia*, 'the books'. Latin-speaking Christians came to see the two testaments as one book and called it *Biblia* (treating it as a singular noun). Hence the English word Bible.[2]

The Languages of the Bible

Having discovered where the word Bible came from we have also found out what many of the sixty-six books that make up the Bible were written on. Either a criss-cross of dried reed bark or treated animal skins. In addition to these, however, further back into the Old Testament, other writing materials were used, including clay or wooden tablets, chips of limestone or broken pieces of pottery.

Now other questions have to be answered. Among them are: In what language were the books of the Bible written? Who wrote them? And when?

Hebrew

Sabra literally means 'cactus flower'. These days, however, it is the term used in Israel for the secularly-minded young Israelis born in Israel who work the *kibbutzim* (fortified villages based around farming but including some industries and crafts).

Sabras are commonly employed by archaeologists in their digs in Israel. Typically *kibbutzim* contain no synagogues and are entirely Hebrew-speaking.

Recently an archaeologist was discussing Deuteronomy (the fifth of the Bible's sixty-six books) with a visitor. He had an ancient fragment of *biblion* with a chapter or two written in the Hebrew in which the bulk of the Old Testament was set down.

'*Ivrit* or modern Hebrew', the archaeologist was saying, 'represents a revival of ancient Hebrew carried out in the early years of the twentieth century by Ben Yehuda. But it is near enough to the original language to enable anyone who reads it to read the ancient Hebrew of the Bible.'

'If that is so,' replied the visitor with some disbelief, 'call the *sabra* working over there and ask her to read your fragment of Deuteronomy. Although she has no religious education she should be able to manage it if what you say is true.'

The sun-bronzed *sabra* was called over. She read every word of the ancient fragment without faltering.

The language of the Old Testament is Hebrew. Despite the hundreds of years over which it was written the linguistic differences between the earlier and later writings are few and of no importance. Today any educated Israeli can read his holy book in its original written-down form.

Aramaic

A few sections of the Old Testament were written in Aramaic. These include chapters in Ezra (4:8-6:18 and 7:12-26) and Daniel (2:4-7:28), and one verse in Jeremiah (10:11). The Aramaic language is closely related to Hebrew.

Aramaic was the language of certain Aramean tribes who migrated from Mesopotamia — between the Tigris and Euphrates rivers — to Syria. In the eighth century BC the Assyrians forcibly deported Arameans to all provinces of their vast empire, thus disseminating the Aramaic language over a wide area. For centuries Jews have repeated the words of

Deuteronomy 26:5: ' " '*A wandering Aramean was my father.*' " '³

The fact that certain sections of the Old Testament were written in Aramaic is accounted for by the fact that, through their wholesale deportation of Arameans, the Assyrians had rendered Aramaic an international language. Hundreds of Aramaic documents from the times of Ezra and Daniel have been found in the Middle East.

In the centuries immediately before the birth of Jesus Aramaic had replaced Hebrew as the language of conversation among the Jews. Nevertheless, when the rabbi read the scrolls and parchments in the synagogue, he read them in Hebrew.

The four New Testament accounts of the life of Jesus indicate that Jesus *read* Hebrew but suggest that, like everyone else, he *spoke* Aramaic. In the story of the raising of Jairus's daughter he said the words 'Little girl, get up,' in Aramaic: '*Talitha cumi*.' When he restored hearing to a deaf man he said the words, 'Open up!' in Aramaic: '*Ephphatha*'. When he shouted from the cross, 'My God, my God, why have you forsaken me?' he said the words in Aramaic: '*Eloi, Eloi, lama sabachthani?*'⁴

Greek

The source of these Aramaic words of Jesus is in the most vivid of the four accounts of the life of Jesus called 'gospels': Mark.

Mark was, in all probability, the young man who was so eager to make his escape from the scene of Jesus' arrest that he left his only garment in the hands of a soldier and ran naked. Later, he was an assistant to missionaries Paul and Barnabas on their journeys.⁵

At some stage it also seems likely that Mark — full name John Mark — spent time with the veteran apostle Peter. Mark would appear to have derived the material upon which he based his gospel from the spoken accounts of Peter. This may explain the vividness and pace of Mark's gospel and the fact that, embedded in its Greek text, are these phrases in Aramaic in the speech of Jesus. The three-and-a-half years Peter had spent in the company of Jesus he could never forget. As he called to mind the events there was, burned into his recollection, the exact words Jesus had used — in the language in which he had used them.

But these tiny spurts of Aramaic are the exception. The New Testament was written in Greek: the *Koine*. A Greek (or a Hellene, the name by which they called themselves) was a man whose language and culture was Greek; and Greece (or Hellas, the name they used) extended as far as Greek language and culture did. The *koine dialektos* was the common speech of the Greek community. It drew on several ancient dialects, especially Attic (the dialect of Athens).

Before Palestine had become part of the Roman Empire, as it was at the time of Jesus, it had been conquered by Alexander the Great. It had been then that the Greek language and culture had begun to take hold. After Alexander's death the eastern portion of his empire was divided between his generals: Ptolemy took Egypt and Palestine; Seleuces took from Thrace to India.

The first Jews to become Hellenized were those who settled in the new city of Alexandria during the rule of Ptolemy. It is likely that it was during this period that the Jewish trading classes and the upper classes in Judea itself began to speak the *koine*.

It was, however, Antiochus III and Antiochus IV, the Seleucid kings, who *enforced* Greek language and culture. The Seleucid capital, Antioch, became a great centre for Greek sport, theatre and pageantry. The extension of the Seleucid Empire to include Palestine provoked a reaction among the Jews.

Two parties emerged, one supporting, one opposing Greek ways. Welcomed by the liberals the Seleucid tyrant Antiochus IV entered Jerusalem in 171BC. He outraged the conservatives and provoked the Revolt of the Maccabees by plundering and desecrating the temple.

But the culture and language for which the Seleucids had stood had bitten deep into Palestine. The language and aspects of the culture outlived the revolts of the period and even conquest by the Romans. Indeed, Caesar Augustus, who presided over the Roman world in the year Jesus was born, was determined to unite it through the diffusion of Greek culture.

The Roman Empire was in fact bilingual. In the Roman army Latin was the official language, but for the rest Greek remained the official tongue in the eastern Mediterranean lands. In Rome itself Greek was spoken at least as much as Latin.

For centuries it appeared that the form of Greek in which the New Testament was written was not only peculiar, but exclusive. Aware that its forms could not be found elsewhere some sarcastically called it 'the language of the Holy Ghost'. Since the 1880s, however, scraps of papyrus and pieces of pottery have been discovered in the Near East, more especially in Egypt. These documents and artefacts have been found to contain 'vernacular Greek', strikingly similar to the Greek of the New Testament. Hence, while New Testament Greek is very dissimilar from the classical Greek spoken and written in *earlier* centuries, it has been proven beyond doubt to have been the form of Greek spoken and written in the *first* century AD, the international language most widely understood: the *koine*.

The very popularity of the form of Greek in which the New Testament was written helps to explain the spread of Christianity in the first century. It was the most thoroughly international language. Hence it was the language most appropriate for the propagation of a vital new message calculated to 'turn the world upside-down'.

References

[1] 2 Timothy 4:9, 13, NIV.
[2] F. F. Bruce, *The Books and the Parchments*, revised edition (1984), pages 2-6.
[3] Deuteronomy 26:5, RSV.
[4] Mark 5:41; 7:34; 15:34.
[5] Mark 14:51, 52; Acts 12:12, 25; 13:5, 13; 15:38-41.

Note

A Greek version of the Old Testament existed at the time of Jesus called the *Septuagint* (from the Latin for seventy).

Ptolemy made Alexandria a great centre of scholarship, building up massive libraries. He invited the Jerusalem high priest, Eleazar, to appoint scholars to translate the Scriptures (the Old Testament, that is) from Hebrew to Greek. Six translators were chosen from each of the twelve tribes of Israel. They went to Alexandria with an especially accurate version of the *Torah* (the Jewish Scriptures).

It was from the fact that seventy-two men were involved in the work of translation that the name *'Septuagint'* was derived.

By the time of Jesus a million Jews lived in Alexandria. They forgot both Hebrew and Aramaic and read the *Torah* in its Greek version. But it was to the Christians, not the Jews, that we owe almost all the manuscript copies of the Septuagint that have survived to our own day. From the first century AD Christians adopted it as their 'authorized version' of the Old Testament.

2

Who wrote the Bible, and when?

Forty men wrote the sixty-six books of the Bible. They did so over approximately 1,600 years.

In the fifteenth century before Christ, Moses, in exceptional circumstances, led the Hebrews out of slavery in Egypt.*

Moses, the author

Moses lived to the age of 120. His life divides into three periods of forty years each.

Born a Hebrew, he was, nevertheless, brought up at the Egyptian court where, for his first forty years, he gained both political and military experience, as well as the best education available in his time.

Abruptly he was forced to flee into exile after an ill-judged (and violent) attack provoked by his sympathy for the enslaved Hebrews, his own people. He spent the second forty-year period working as a wilderness shepherd in Midian.

It was after that that he assumed the role of the great liberator of his people. Estimates of the total number of those he led from Egypt around the Sinai Peninsula to the very borders of the land they were to occupy, vary. Two million is not an unrealistic figure. This third period, in which Moses earned the reputation 'the greatest leader of men the world has ever known', also lasted forty years.

Christian preacher Dwight Moody said: 'The first forty

---

*See Chapter 19 on the dating of Moses and the Exodus.

years of Moses' life he was becoming a somebody. The second forty years of his life he was becoming a nobody. And the third forty years of his life he was proving to the world what God can do with somebody who is a nobody.'

In fact, it is likely that Moses accomplished more in the middle phase of his life than learning how to be a nobody and tend sheep in the wilderness.

When, following Moses' death, Joshua led the Hebrews into the land west of the Jordan, it was with the admonition, '*Do not let this Book of the Law depart from your mouth*.' Soon he was gathering his migrant nation together. Half of them swarmed over the slopes of Mount Gerazim, half over Mount Ebal. (Between the two mountains was the site of what would become the city of Shechem, now Nablus.) There '*Joshua read all the words of the law . . . just as it is written in the Book of the Law. There was not a word of all that Moses had commanded that Joshua did not read to the whole assembly of Israel*.' Much later Joshua was still exhorting the people '*to obey all that is written in the Book of . . . Moses*'.[1]

The Book (or, books) of Moses are accepted as having been the *Torah* or *Pentateuch*, the first five books of the Old Testament (Genesis, Exodus, Leviticus, Numbers and Deuteronomy). King David, whose reign began *circa* 1050 BC (that is, 500 years or so *after* Moses) accepted his authorship of the Pentateuch.[2] Between the golden age of empire under David and Solomon and the destruction of Jerusalem by the Babylonians in 586 BC two other kings — Amaziah and Josiah — (by implication) accepted Moses' authorship.[3] Years later, after the Exile, Ezra and Nehemiah did likewise. The five books of Moses, often termed 'the *Book* of Moses', receive seven references in the second book of Chronicles, seventeen references in each of Ezra and Nehemiah, and one reference in Malachi.

The first of his five books — Genesis — Moses would appear

to have in part written, in part collated during the middle period of his life, the period in Midian.

Exodus extends the narrative begun in Genesis. In certain statements Moses is specifically named as having been the author of it. The activities of Moses as a chronicler, as well as law-giver and codifier of law, are actually mentioned.[4] The skills used by Moses in authoring Exodus, Numbers, Leviticus and Deuteronomy in this third period of his life had almost certainly been acquired during the higher education of Egypt to which he had been exposed in the first part of his life.[5] Jesus accepted that Moses had written Exodus.[6] Leviticus is the core of what Jesus called 'the law of Moses'.[7] Elsewhere he implied that Moses had been a prolific writer.[8]

The fifth book of the Pentateuch, Deuteronomy, was clearly edited and added to since it incorporates the story of Moses' own death! Nevertheless, Jesus and the early Christian leaders, by their words and the use they made of it, clearly accepted Moses as the main author of Deuteronomy.[9]

There is a strong tradition in both Judaism and Christianity that Moses also authored the profoundly reflective and beautifully poetical book of Job. And, further, that he did so during the middle (Midianite) period of his life. Scholars have attacked the tradition that Moses authored the prose-poetry that makes up much of this book, pointing out the way in which the style contrasts with the style of much of the Pentateuch.

This contrast in both style and content with Moses' other books may have an explanation. Though he married and fathered a family during this period, the nature of his occupation would have given Moses ample time for reflection. The mental apparatus, honed and refined in Egypt's best universities, could begin to process some of the great problems of life. *Par excellence* Job is the book that grapples the problem, Why is there pain, disease and death in a world over which an all-powerful, all-loving God presides? When Moses soars into the realms of poetry is he sitting under the sharp desert stars and constellations?

' *"Can you bind the chains of the Pleiades?*
  Or loose the cords of Orion?"
  "Can you send forth lightnings, that they may go
  and say to you, 'Here we are'?
  Who has put wisdom in the clouds,
  or given understanding to the mists?
  Who can number the clouds by wisdom?
  Or who can tilt the waterskins of the heavens,
  when the dust runs into a mass
  and the clods cleave fast together?"
  "Who has cleft a channel for the torrents of rain,
  and a way for the thunderbolt,
  to bring rain on a land where no man is,
  on the desert on which there is no man;
  to satisfy the waste and desolate land,
  and to make the ground put forth grass?" '[10]

If the author of Job was indeed Moses, he was using Job's story to answer the question, How can my people be exploited as slaves in Egypt and God still be God? Through the various 'speakers' in the Book, Moses is exploring alternative views of the nature of God, and reaching the 'loving, merciful' model to which most Jews and Christians adhere. The theological framework of Job leans on Genesis (the other book Moses wrote in Midian) with its account of the Fall, the origin of sin, and its depiction of a personal, malevolent devil.

Uniformity and diversity

Even if you accept that only *one* of the six books attributed to Moses was actually written by him, you have accepted that the Bible began to be written 3,500 years ago. And, since there can be little doubt that the last book of the New Testament was written around the end of the first century AD, you have also accepted that the Bible was 1,600 years in the writing. Having accepted that, you cannot but marvel at the uniformity of thought, narrative and revelation. Marvel too at the absence of conflict between the messages written by forty different individuals, from an immense diversity of backgrounds, education, historical periods and geographical locations.

Consider the diversity of occupation among the men who wrote the Bible.

A general. The continuing narrative of the book of Joshua, though written in the third person, is widely accepted as having been written by Joshua himself. This does not exclude the possibility of additions after his death, or that Joshua collated part of the narrative and actually wrote other parts. Joshua, it will be recalled, was a general.

A priest. It is conjectured (no more) that the book of Judges was written by Samuel; and fairly generally accepted that the first twenty-four chapters of the first book of Samuel were written by Samuel. Samuel was a priest.

A scribe. The remainder of the books of Samuel were written by Nathan and Gad (see 1 Chronicles 29:29). These men were prophets and scribes.

The historical narratives of the two books of Kings and the two books of Chronicles represent the compilation of a variety of historical sources, but it is impossible to tell who undertook this painstaking task for the books of Kings. However, insofar as the two books of Chronicles, Ezra and Nehemiah are closely related to one another in language, style and general point of view, it may be assumed that there was one author. The fact that Chronicles ends in the middle of a sentence — which is completed in the opening verses of Ezra — may indicate that Ezra was the author. Similarly there is a close relationship between the books of Ezra and Nehemiah; the ancients saw them as one book, not two. Evidence in the books themselves suggest they were written, or at the very least completed in the period of Persian domination, *circa* 400 BC. The author, Ezra, was a priest of a priestly family.

A king. The book of Psalms is the hymnbook of the Bible. Hence there is a great diversity of authors. Most notable among them was David, a shepherd who became a king. Another notable psalmist was Asaph, a musician.

Internal evidence in the book of Proverbs identifies King Solomon as its author. There is little doubt that Solomon also wrote Ecclesiastes and the book known as the Song of Solomon. Solomon was a king-scholar.

The authors of the two Old Testament books bearing the names of women, Ruth and Esther, have never been satisfactorily identified.

Were there two Isaiahs? The fact that the book of Isaiah breaks at the end of chapter 39 and appears, thereafter, to be addressing a different group of people with a very different message has led scholars to believe that Isaiah represents two books. Indeed, there has been talk of Isaiah and *Deutero*-Isaiah. Up to the end of chapter 39 Isaiah is addressing his message to the people prior to the fall of Jerusalem to the Babylonians. From the beginning of chapter 40 the message is clearly being addressed to a different group of people in a different time zone. In the first 39 chapters Babylon is the great menace of the future. From the beginning of chapter 40 Babylon is in the past and Persia rules. Some scholars assume that the same man, Isaiah, spoke the message of repentance and denunciation prior to the exile; *and* the message of hope and comfort to those under Persian overlordship who were about to be liberated and to return to Jerusalem. It is assumed that this was part of the prophetic privilege; that an all-knowing God permitted Isaiah to see beyond the doom and destruction of Jerusalem to the time when the exile was almost over. That being the case, Isaiah was permitted to view events 150 years beyond his own time and (in writing) to speak to the people of that time, many years after his own death. The prophet Isaiah was, without question, an educated Hebrew aristocrat of the royal line.

Prophets, slaves, herdsmen — and a prime minister. Some of the prophetic books of the Old Testament were written by 'professional' prophets. Among them is Jeremiah. Jeremiah, however, had the assistance of his trusted secretary, Baruch. The authorship of the book Lamentations also belongs to Jeremiah. At all events the arguments against his authorship are most unconvincing.

The long, intricate, and at times puzzling book of Ezekiel was written by a (highly educated) Hebrew slave working as part of a slave gang in the mud flats of the plains of Babylon near the Kebah Canal. Hence the Bible can be said to count among its contributors a slave.

The book of Daniel, by contrast, was written by the man who bears its name; a man who, in turn, served Babylonian and Persian kings in the position of first minister. Given the fact that he was a Hebrew exile and nevertheless assumed a position of such great prominence over so long a period, it must be assumed that Daniel was a statesman of great wisdom and massive intellect.

Among the minor prophets is Hosea, a 'professional' prophet, though a rather exceptional one: he filled the prophetic office for a period in excess of seventy years. Joel is also simply known as a prophet. Amos is designated as a herdsman and a gatherer of sycamore fruit (sycamore figs). Despite a mention in the book of Kings nothing is known about Jonah's occupation beyond the fact that he was a spokesman for God. Micah was a younger contemporary of Isaiah, but we do not know his occupation. His style suggests a rugged, simple, forthright peasant farmer. Zephaniah had a royal heredity; he was descended from Hezekiah. Zechariah was probably a priest.

When Malachi, the last prophet of the Old Testament, came to deliver his message, the period of the exile was a distant memory. The abuses he condemns are the same as those during Nehemiah's long absences at the Persian court. It is thus highly probable that Malachi set down his message *circa* 425 BC. Regrettably we know nothing for certain of his occupation, though it may be conjectured that he was a priest.

The four gospel writers. The New Testament contains a similar diversity of authors. The gospel writers — Matthew, Mark, Luke and John — were, respectively, an officer of the Inland Revenue, an early Christian eager to set down the recollections of his elders, a physician, and the mystical, well-loved disciple of Jesus.

A tentmaker — and an intellectual. Paul, who wrote most of the letters contained in the New Testament, was a tent maker by trade. From time to time he practised the trade. In addition, however, he was a theologian, an intellectual and, prior to his conversion to Christianity, one of the leaders of the Jews.

Peter, the fisherman — and writer. By contrast Peter was a fisherman. The author of the letter of James was no less than the brother of Jesus himself, in contemporary usage a 'bishop'.

A motley collection to produce so many books with such great diversity of style but with equally great uniformity of message and purpose.

When were the gospels written?

Of the four gospels, Mark was undoubtedly written first. How can we know that?

Because, as we read the first three gospels, it becomes clear that Matthew and Luke borrowed heavily from Mark. Some stories are told in exactly the same words; the teaching of Jesus is presented in an almost identical way. Mark can be divided into 105 sections. Of these, ninety-three occur in Matthew, and eighty-one in Luke. Only four are not included either in Matthew or in Luke. Mark has 661 verses; Matthew has 1,068 verses; Luke has 1,149 verses. Of Mark's 661 verses, Matthew reproduces no fewer than 606. Occasionally he alters the wording slightly; but he reproduces 51 per cent of Mark's actual words. Of Mark's 661 verses, Luke reproduces 320, and 53 per cent of Mark's actual words. Of the fifty-five verses of Mark which Matthew does not reproduce, thirty-one are found in Luke. Hence there are only twenty-four verses in Mark which do not occur in Matthew and Luke.

Obviously Matthew and Luke were based on Mark, and Mark was the first of the gospels.

Hence Mark is the 'essential gospel'; Matthew and Luke even follow Mark's order of events. There is a fast pace and a gripping realism in Mark. Over and over again he includes little vivid details in his narrative; evidence that Mark was basing his narrative on an eye-witness account — almost certainly that of Peter.

The fact that Matthew, Mark and Luke have so much in common has led scholars to refer to them as the 'Synoptic Gospels'. (*Synoptic* comes from the Greek words which mean 'to see together'.)

The 'Q' source. There are, however, 200 additional verses in Matthew and Luke, not present in Mark. These are concerned with what Jesus *said*, whereas the main preoccupation of Mark was with what Jesus *did*. Scholars have assumed that Matthew and Luke had recourse to another source book in addition to Mark. They have called it Q (short for *Quelle*, the German word for *source*). This other source — Q — was clearly a source book of the teachings of Jesus. Beyond that no one knows anything about it or has ever been able to find it.

The Gospel for the Jews. Matthew's gospel is essentially the gospel written to convince the Jews that Jesus was the Messiah. Matthew eagerly demonstrates that all of the prophecies of the Old Testament were fulfilled in Jesus and that, therefore, *he must be* the Messiah. Matthew's gospel is also preoccupied with the relationship between Jesus and the Jews, whether positive or negative. Matthew's concern at the outset is to prove that Jesus was a direct descendant of King David.

The Gospel for the Gentiles. Luke's gospel was essentially a gospel written for the gentiles. He demonstrates tremendous care in setting out the events of the gospel narrative in the context of secular history. Before describing the birth of Jesus he names the Roman Caesar, the king of the Jews and the governor of Syria in that year. Luke is even more careful to date the emergence of John the Baptist. (Luke 3:1, 2). In addition, Luke wrote the best Greek of the New Testament.

The intimate Gospel. John's gospel is very different from the other three. When John's gospel was written it is clear that the gospels of Matthew, Mark and Luke were already available. Perhaps John, the disciple who had been closest to Jesus, read the other gospel accounts in his old age, and thought that before it was too late he must set down on paper his own specific, intimate recollections of the life and the teaching of Jesus.

John omits much of what Matthew, Mark and Luke had already set down. What was the point of repeating it? That was not his purpose. But he knew that there was much that they had omitted. And that he was eager to include. Only John tells of the marriage feast at Cana, the introduction of the new birth teaching to Nicodemus, of the woman of Samaria, of the raising of Lazarus, of the way Jesus washed his disciples' feet, and the wonderful 'Upper Room Sermon' of John 13-17.

In John's gospel each disciple assumes a personality of his

own; John had known them all well. Of course, in informing Mark, Peter had known them equally well. But the intention of Peter and Mark in compiling their gospel was simply to provide a brief, fast-moving account of the life of Jesus. John, by contrast, takes much of that account for granted but seeks to make the personalities come alive. All the gospel writers mention the miracle of the feeding of the 5,000, but only John mentions that the boy's loaves were *barley* loaves. In the story of the calming of the sea only John mentions that the disciples had rowed between three and four miles from the shoreline. In recounting the crucifixion only John observed that four soldiers were gambling for the seamless robe of his master.

Written in fifty years. The New Testament books were, in the main, written between AD 50 and AD 100. Old Testament books, it will be recalled, were written over a much longer period.

Clearly Mark was written prior to the death of Peter. Since this occurred between AD 64 and AD 66 most authorities have assumed that Mark's gospel was set down at some time between AD 55 and AD 64.

Matthew's gospel is more difficult to date; there is no consensus of agreement among scholars.

However Luke who, in addition to his gospel, wrote the book of Acts and addressed both books to Theophilus, gives us a number of clues to work on. In some passages in the book of Acts he is writing in the third person; in others he is writing in the first person, making it clear that *he* was actually present. Luke wrote his gospel *before* he wrote the book of Acts. The book of Acts breaks off suddenly, for no logical reason. The simplest explanation for this is that Luke had no more to tell; his narrative had reached the present. Since 'the present' was the beginning of Paul's first imprisonment in Rome (*circa*

AD 61-63), Acts was obviously written before AD 63 — and Luke's gospel even earlier.

John's writing almost certainly took place entirely in the 90s. His three letters towards the end of the New Testament were written to combat heresies that were entering the church at that time. This dates them to the late 90s or AD 100. John's gospel has been dated to the same period. John's Book of Revelation — in which we find him peering down the corridor of the future towards an end-time age and an apocalypse — was written from his exile on the island of Patmos (his other books were written in Ephesus). On the evidence of historians, including Eusebius, we know that John's banishment to Patmos occurred during the imperial reign of Domitian. Hence, rather surprisingly, it would appear that the Book of Revelation was written before John's gospel and three letters: AD 95 or even earlier.

Paul's letters. Most of the New Testament is taken up with letters, and most of these letters were written by Paul. Paul, whose original name was Saul, began as a member of the Jewish establishment and a persecutor of the Christians. His conversion to Christianity was the most dramatic of all and occurred on the road to Damascus.

After his conversion Paul went on a number of 'missionary journeys'. In each of these a team of assistants accompanied him. Together they raised up a number of churches and encountered fierce persecution. In the main the letters were written after the churches had been established and from some considerable distance. They were written because of feedback received by Paul with regard to problems occurring in the churches he had founded. Paul wrote his letters, almost entirely, to address specific problems.

For example, when Paul was in Ephesus in AD 55 he heard that all was not well with the church in Corinth. Corinth was one of the greatest trading and commercial centres in the ancient world. But that was not its only claim to notoriety. The term 'Corinthian' was used throughout the Greek-speaking world for a man entirely given over to drunkenness and immorality. The city was dominated by a hill and atop the hill was the Temple of Aphrodite, the goddess of love. One thousand prostitute priestesses were attached to that temple and plied their trade in the streets of the city. This atmosphere of corruption had permeated the Corinthian church. Immorality was rife, the grace of God was being taken for granted, and the gifts of the Holy Spirit were being misused.

When Paul wrote to Galatia in the winter of AD 57/58 he was on his third missionary journey. In Galatia the very core of the gospel he had preached was under attack. The attackers were termed 'the Judaizers'. If their attack had succeeded, Christianity would have become no more than a sect of Judaism. In a sense their problem was the opposite of the one in Corinth. They wanted men to believe that they were saved by a rigorous observance of every detail of the law. In effect they believed that before a man could become a Christian he must first become a Jew with all that that implied. This was Paul's opportunity to reassert the essence of his gospel: salvation was a free gift from God to those who would accept the sacrifice of his Son Jesus Christ on Calvary.

The letter to the Romans was different from the others. When he wrote it Paul had never been to Rome and was, therefore, addressing no specific problems. That is why the book of Romans is the nearest thing in the New Testament to a systematic exposition of Christian theology. Hence it has been regarded as the most important book in the New Testament. It has been said that every revival in the history of Christianity has resulted from a study of the book of Romans. Certainly the Protestant Reformation, led by Martin Luther, came as a direct result of Luther's understanding of justification by faith in Romans. In writing to the Roman church from Corinth in AD 58 Paul was setting out the very essence of his belief in order to foster a strong church which, he may have hoped, would help him achieve his stated aim of evangelizing Spain.

Paul wrote personal letters too. Among them were the letters to Timothy and Titus. His second letter to Timothy is likely to have been his last. It was in this letter that he asked for his warm coat, his books and his parchments before the onset of winter (2 Timothy 4:9, 13). He was beheaded in AD 67.

The last writer. But, while Paul was the major contributor to the New Testament, and the writer to whom the Christian church owes its greatest debt, it was John in the final years of the century who was to produce the last-written of the New Testament books. They were his distinctive gospel, three letters, and the Book of Revelation. John, the beloved disciple of Jesus, is believed to have been the only apostle to die a natural death. He was the last of those forty writers whose collective works written over a period of 1,600 years have come to be known by Christians as the Bible.

References
[1] Joshua 1:8; 8:33-35; 23:6, NIV.
[2] 1 Kings 2:3.
[3] 2 Kings 14:6; 22:8-23:24.
[4] Exodus 17:14; 24:4; Numbers 33:2.
[5] Acts 7:22.
[6] Mark 12:26 quotes Exodus 3:6.
[7] Luke 24:44.
[8] John 5:46, 47.
[9] Matthew 19:7, 8 (Deuteronomy 24:1); Mark 12:19 (Deuteronomy 25:5); John 1:17; 7:19 (Deuteronomy 4:44); John 1:45; Acts 3:22 (Deuteronomy 18:15); Hebrews 10:28 (Deuteronomy 17:2-7).
[10] These quotations are all taken from Job 38.

3

How the books of the Bible were brought together

We have looked at the people who wrote the sixty-six books of the Bible, where possible given the approximate dates *when* each book was written and, therefore, been able to estimate the total period between the time when the first book was penned and the last book completed.

But how were all these books brought together to be designated 'holy' or 'special'?

We need to answer this question in two halves because the Bible is divided into two 'testaments', Old and New.

Books that were different

The word 'holy' crops up again and again in the books of both the Old and the New Testaments. Many things are declared to be 'holy': certain books, places, the temple, to give but a few examples. The basic meaning of this word 'holy' in both Hebrew and Greek is 'different'. God is declared to be supremely the Holy One because he is different from anyone else.

To Christians the Bible is a holy book. In fact, as we have seen, it is a veritable library of books. How did the thirty-nine books of the Old Testament and the twenty-seven books of the New Testament come to be considered especially 'holy' or 'different'?

We have already established that the Bible was, to say the least, *unusual*. The forty men who wrote it were separated from one another by hundreds of years and hundreds of miles, belonged to a great many different walks of life, had every conceivable level of education from the highest to the lowest, and many diverse personality types. We have seen that among them were, on the one hand, herdsmen, shepherds, soldiers, fishermen and tent makers; and, on the other, kings, legislators, statesmen, courtiers, priests and physicians.

Inevitably their literary styles reflected their very great differences. Some were writing law, others religious poetry, still others history, some lyrical prose, others lyrical poetry, some were writing in parables and allegories, others biographies or personal memoirs and diaries, some were writing prophecy, and still others quite simply, personal correspondence.

With all this tremendous diversity how were the sixty-six books deemed to be sufficiently 'different' or 'holy' to be included in what is called the 'canon' of the Bible?

The first thing to understand is that no individual or committee of individuals compiled the Bible. The Bible *grew*. This principle applies to both the Old and New Testaments. Over many centuries the books grew to be accepted as holy scripture. To chronicle that growth is to be made aware of the working of a hand and a mind that were not human. The unifying principle which makes the Bible holy, different, a living whole, is this: Christ himself, the bringer of salvation. As we watch the process by which the books were written and grew to acceptance we receive a sense that the One who was the unifying principle, the bringer of salvation, the source of inspiration, was also at work.

Books of the Old Testament. A great teacher once wrote: 'Few realize that the Church of Christ possesses a higher warrant for her canon of the Old Testament than she does for her canon of the New.'[1]

The point he was making was that Jesus quoted and attributed authority to all parts of the Old Testament and, to his disciples after his resurrection, said that everything that had happened to him was a fulfilment of Old Testament prophecy. And Messianic prophecy was scattered throughout the Old Testament. Of course, because it had yet to be written, he could not give similar weight to the authority of the New Testament.

The Old Testament books are usually divided into four sections: the Pentateuch (the books of Moses); the historical books (Joshua to Esther); the five books of poetry and ethics (Job to the Song of Solomon); and the books of the prophets (Isaiah to Malachi).

In popular text books the assertion is made that this collection of books was debated and declared 'canonical' at the Council of Jamnia which met in AD110. This is an untrue statement.

The work of forming what became known as the Old Testament was begun as early as 450BC and was undertaken by Ezra. Most scholars now accept that, by the time of Christ, the Old Testament existed in the form outlined above.

True enough, there *was* considerable discussion about the canon of scripture among rabbis following the fall of Jerusalem in AD70. A rabbi called Yochanan ben Zakkai obtained written permission from the Roman authorities to convene the Council of Jamnia in order to discuss the canon of scripture. However, the debate at that council simply centred around four books that were considered to be 'marginal': Proverbs, Ecclesiastes, the Song of Solomon and Esther. When the pros and cons with regard to these four books had been discussed it was decided to include them within the canon along with the rest of what we know as the Old Testament books. In fact, they could have done little else; 'the books which they decided to acknowledge as canonical were already generally accepted, although questions had been raised about them. Those (books) which they refused to admit had never been included. They did not expel from the canon any book which had previously been admitted.'[2]

The Council of Jamnia did not invest the books of the Bible with authority by including them in some sacred list. They were included in that list — the *canon* — because they were already acknowledged as God-inspired, authoritative, and had been, in most cases, for a number of centuries.

A contemporary of Christ, Philo of Alexandria, accepted the Old Testament canon in the form in which it is accepted today. The same is true of first century Josephus Flavius. The earliest list of Old Testament books extant was drawn up by Melito, Bishop of Sardis, about AD 170 and is preserved by Eusebius in the fourth volume of his *Ecclesiastical History*.[3]

Books of the New Testament. There are three categories of New Testament books: the narrative books (the four gospels and the Acts); the letters; and the apocalyptic book of Revelation which stands out on its own.

Although it took only fifty years to write the New Testament it took far longer for it to assume the form that it has today. Not until AD 367 do we find the New Testament books listed in exactly their present form. The list is contained in an Easter letter written by a Christian bishop, Athanasius. He was advising the flock as to which books were 'in the Bible' and which were not.

In the two-and-a-half centuries or so between the completion of the last book of the New Testament and the list of Athanasius there had been much discussion as to which books should and should not be included in the canon. The Old Testament formed the Scriptures of the earliest Christians; gradually some Christian writings were placed on a par with it, 'not by any decree of a Council . . . but by the common agreement of the faithful; the spiritual intuition of the Church came slowly to decide which of its writings should be regarded as "canonical" '.[4]

What brought about 'the common agreement of the faithful'? What informed 'the spiritual intuition of the Church'?

The books discarded from the Old Testament canon came to be called the *Apocrypha*. A further group of wrongly-attributed books — called the *Pseudepigrapha* — were also discarded. The Apocrypha contained history and wise sayings. The Pseudepigrapha contained a lot of magic and a little history. As we examine the books discarded from the New Testament canon — the New Testament 'Apocrypha' — again we sense the presence of supernatural guidance.

The books included were those accepted as God-inspired and proven in their ability to help men and to make Christ known. They were acknowledged to have been written by men close to Jesus and involved in the great first-century adventure which took the Christian Gospel to the limits of the then known world.

A Greek contemporary of Athanasius spoke of 'the echo of a great soul' and professed to hear this echo in the canonical New Testament books. William Barclay has said: 'The ring of sublimity is to be found in the New Testament books. They carry their greatness on their faces. *They are self-evidencing.*' When W. E. Gladstone was asked why he believed the Bible was inspired, he answered, simply; '*It finds me.*'

In *Ring of Truth: A Translator's Testimony* (1967) J. B. Phillips writes that, when he came to compare the New Testament books 'with the writings which were excluded from the New Testament by the early "Fathers" I can only admire their wisdom. Probably most people have not had the opportunity to read the apocryphal "gospels" and "epistles", although every scholar has. I can only say here that in such writings we live in a world of magic and make-believe, of myth and fancy. In the whole task of translating the New Testament I never for one moment, however provoked and challenged I might be, felt that I was being swept away into a world of spookiness, witchcraft and magical powers such as abound in the books rejected from the New Testament. It was the sustained down-to-earth faith of the New Testament writers which conveyed to me that inexpressible sense of the genuine and the authentic.' (Page 95.)

The 'self-evidencing' point is made most powerfully when one reads the books that almost got into the New Testament but did not; books that were intended by their authors to be accepted, but were not.

In the second century a number of books were written called 'infancy gospels'. The four gospels of the canon provide little detail on the first three decades of the life of Jesus prior to the commencement of his public ministry. These infancy gospels were intended to 'fill in the gaps'.

The so-called 'gospel of Thomas' is supposed to give a record of the infancy of Jesus.

The child Jesus, while at play, is represented as creating live sparrows out of clay, and of striking dead a small child who 'ran and crashed against his shoulder'. Jesus the apprenticed carpenter is depicted stretching wooden beams like elastic and exercising an assortment of magical powers to no practical purpose.

No one could possibly mistake this for Scripture; nor have they. Scripture is *self-evidencing*. When you read the gospels by the side of these books there is no question as to why some are 'in' and others, without argument, 'out'. The line is clear cut. There is no room for debate.

Immense care was taken to ensure that the people who had authored the books that were accepted into the canon had known Jesus. The hallmark of these men was that they were concerned to demonstrate that Jesus was not a person who *did* things, but that he is a person who *does* things. That Jesus is alive.

In the book of Acts every single sermon finishes with the

fact of the resurrection. For the New Testament Jesus was above all the living Christ. Because the four gospel writers were speaking about the living Christ they gave a vastly disproportionate amount of space to the last week prior to his crucifixion and resurrection. This was their central concern. The central fact of Christianity, of Christian theology is the death and resurrection of Jesus Christ. The books where this was not the central concern were quite simply either not considered or deliberately excluded from the canon.

'We may well believe', says Professor F. F. Bruce, 'that those early Christians acted by a wisdom higher than their own in this matter, not only in what they accepted, but in what they rejected.' 'What is particularly important to notice is that the New Testament canon was not demarcated by the arbitrary decree of any Church Council. When at last a Church Council — the Synod of Hippo in AD 393 — listed the twenty-seven books of the New Testament, it did not confer upon them any authority which they did not already possess, but simply recorded their previously established canonicity.'[5]

In short, the process by which the Books of the New Testament came to be accepted was, in all essential respects, the same process by which the Books of the Old Testament came to be accepted. Thus these two books — the Bible of the apostles and the Bible the apostles wrote — together came to comprise what Christians accept as the written Word of God.

References
[1] G. A. Smith, *Modern Criticism and the Preaching of the Old Testament* (1901), page 5.
[2] F. F. Bruce, *The Books and the Parchments* (1984), page 89.
[3] Ibid, pages 89-92.
[4] G. W. H. Lampe (ed), *The Cambridge History of the Bible*, volume 2 (1969), page 42.
[5] F. F. Bruce, *op cit*, pages 103, 104.

BATTLE
FOR
THE
BIBLE

4

Surviving the centuries

We have seen how the Bible came to be written and approximately when. We have looked at the men who wrote it and glimpsed the reasons why it was written. We have traced the process by which the sixty-six books came to be accepted as the Holy Bible.

But the last book of the Bible was completed by the end of the first century AD.

Question: How did the sixty-six books survive the centuries, *especially* the centuries before Johann Gutenberg of Mainz invented printing (in the 1430s)?

Answer: It was laboriously copied out by hand thousands of times by generations of copyists.

Obvious conclusion: Since this process had been going on for well over a thousand years before the invention of printing, surely the whole text must be riddled with mistakes and inaccuracies made by the copyists. And these mistakes and inaccuracies could only have been perpetuated when the Bible began to be printed.

Old Testament under fire

Controversy over the reliability and accuracy of the Bible came to a head in the eighteenth century, the Age of Reason. It particularly focused around the Old Testament. The Hebrew text of the Old Testament was based on manuscripts that were produced as recently as *the ninth century AD*. They were the earliest manuscripts known.

German scholars more than others were adamant: The Bible

could *not* be trusted. Friedrich Delitzsch spoke for scores of eighteenth, nineteenth and twentieth century scholars when, in 1921, he wrote that the biblical text had experienced *a degree of corruption beyond our wildest imagination.*[1]

Until the 1940s such views represented the received wisdom. In 1939 ancient manuscript authority Sir Frederic Kenyon wrote about the Masoretes who, for many centuries, had taken it upon themselves to copy out the Scriptures. The very oldest of their manuscripts dated from around AD 900. It was, he said, most regrettable that generations of Jewish rabbis for more than a thousand years had viewed copies of holy Scripture with such superstitious veneration that, as soon as they had become old and worn, they had reverently buried them. Hence the absence of any Old Testament manuscripts to pre-date the Masoretic texts of the AD 900s. By contrast, much earlier manuscripts of the New Testament survived and could be depended upon. The 'great and all-important question' was this: 'Does this Hebrew text (of the Old Testament), which we call Masoretic, and which we have shown to descend from the texts drawn up about AD 100, faithfully represent the Hebrew text as originally written by the authors of the Old Testament books?'[2]

Kenyon was charitable. At least he put it as a question. Most scholars presented an answer to the question similar to that of Friedrich Delitzsch: In the 1,300 years between the completion of Malachi and the oldest surviving Masoretic text the Old Testament had been garbled beyond recognition.

Question: What *could* devout Jewish and Christian scholars do?

Answer: Come up with some inconclusive arguments before withdrawing in embarrassment. Among themselves they admitted: True enough, it was not reasonable to assume that, having used up the ink of thousands of copyists over ten centuries, the Old Testament Scriptures had remained unchanged.

What was known of these copyists? Their habits, their reputation for accuracy?

The Masoretes

The Masoretes were fanatics in their passion for accuracy,
obsessive in their devotion to tradition. The name Masoretes
came from the Hebrew word *masoroh*: *tradition*. The tradition
to which they were devoted was that of passing down and
recopying the sacred manuscripts across the centuries with the
highest possible degree of accuracy and, as Hebrew ceased to
be a living vernacular, adding punctuation marks and vowel
points to guide those who read the Scriptures in the
synagogues.

In the years up to the 1940s Jewish and Christian scholars,
wishing to defend the accuracy of the Old Testament, made
much of what was known of the reputation for accuracy of
the Masoretes.

The scoffers asserted that the defenders of the Old Testament
were assuming too much. The earliest manuscripts of the *New*
Testament dated from the third and fourth centuries. The
earliest manuscripts of the *Old* Testament were as recent as
the *Codex of the Prophets* at Leningrad dated AD 916. The
'Codex' simply means 'written manuscript in book form' (as
opposed to written manuscripts in scroll form). Both Oxford
University and Leningrad had a *complete* codex of the Hebrew
Old Testament but both dated from as late as the eleventh
century. In a synagogue in Aleppo, it was said, there was a
codex of the whole Hebrew Bible dating from the tenth century, but this disappeared in the Jewish War of Independence
1948 (and did not re-appear until many years after).

Christian and Jewish scholars made much of the fragments
of the Old Testament manuscripts dating from earlier periods.

There was the *Nash Papyrus* (which contained a portion
of the ten commandments). Some authorities claimed that

this fragment of a biblical scroll was pre-Christian.

Christians would point out, in addition, that *circa* AD 400 Jerome, working in a Bethlehem cave, had translated the Old Testament from Hebrew to Latin (and the New Testament from Greek to Latin). Jerome's Latin Bible — the 'Vulgate' — was the only Bible in use in Christendom for a thousand years. Jerome's Old Testament *must* represent some kind of guarantee of the accuracy of transmission, they would argue. But, the more scholars probed the Vulgate, the more errors in translation they uncovered. . . .

The same was true of the Syriac (or Christian Aramaic) Bible which had been in use as early as AD 400. . . .

So the defenders of the accuracy of the Old Testament found themselves leaning heavily on the reputation of the Masoretes — and faith.

Rabbi Akiba and his 'Great Work'

When Roman General Titus left Jerusalem in smouldering ruins in AD 70 he may have assumed that the mass slaughter that accompanied Jerusalem's fall, and the mass slaughter that had preceded it in his Galilean campaign, had crushed Judaism for ever.

When Roman General Silva, after the AD 70-73 seige, entered the Zealot mountain stronghold of Masada to find that Eliezer, son of Yair, with his supporters, had committed mass suicide — *he* may have assumed that he had witnessed the last stand of Judaism.

When Roman Emperor Hadrian levelled Old Jerusalem in AD 135 and built a Roman city — *Aelia Capitolina* — over its base, he knew that scattered groups of hard-pressed Jews were to be found in Palestine and elsewhere; but is unlikely to have perceived them as in any way significant.

The Jewish religion had died with the destruction of its temple in AD 70.

Or had it?

Judaism lived on without its temple and its system of sacrifices.

Judaism became a religion of sacred writings — and of scholars whose work was to preserve, copy and interpret them.

In AD 110 Yohanan ben Zakkai chaired the Council of Jamnia. Rabbi Akiba ben Joseph (AD 55-137) became its most prominent member. Having grown up as an illiterate, orphan shepherd boy his giant intellect had been stretched by ben Zakkai at the rabbinical school in Jamnia. Akiba sought to rally his shattered people around the sacred Scriptures. They were all that was left for the chosen people.

Akiba, based in Tverya (Tiberias), a city by Galilee, worked to standardize the Hebrew text. All subsequent copies and translations were based on Akiba's standardized text.

A group of scholars clustered around Akiba at Tiberias. A similar group of rabbis were working on similar projects in Babylonia. In addition to working on the (Old Testament) Scriptures, they worked to *interpret* the Scriptures.

Their chief concern was the *Torah* (or Law), the five books of Moses. They sought to take the broad principles of the Law and apply them, in an infinity of ingenious ways, to all the complex situations of life. As a result the Tiberias scholars produced the *Mishnah*. The rabbis in Babylonia produced the *Gemara*. The two parts were joined together circa AD 500 to become the *Talmud*.

Well before this time the groups of Jewish scholars in Tiberias and Babylonia had developed a high standard (tradition, *masorah*) of professionalism to preserve the purity of the biblical manuscripts they were copying. They devised a complicated system of safeguards against mistakes. Though always staying close to Akiba's standardized text, they *did*, from time to time, 'consider variant readings found in the manuscripts at their disposal'.[3]

It was the widespread reverence for the Masoretic text of the Old Testament that led biblical scholars who lived centuries after the Masoretes had completed their work to be completely satisfied with its authenticity.

The last Masoretic family was that of ben Asher of Tiberias. It is likely that they were responsible for the Masoretic *Codex of the Prophets* that survives in Leningrad.

'The all-important question'

The reputation of the Masoretes notwithstanding, however, the 'great, indeed all-important question' when Sir Frederic Kenyon completed the fourth edition of *Our Bible and the Ancient Manuscripts* in 1939 was: Could modern Bible scholars *really* believe that the Masoretes had preserved the thirty-nine books of the Old Testament free from error through eight centuries of copying?

Most answered, No. Much of what was taught about the Masoretes was myth, anyway, it was alleged. Far more likely — and a great deal more popular — was the establishment view epitomized by Friedrich Delitzsch that the biblical text had been bowdlerized and corrupted 'beyond our wildest imagination'.

One day in 1947 that establishment view was unassailable. The next day it came tumbling down.

What brought it down was a stone thrown by a young bedouin in the vicinity of the Dead Sea.

References
[1] Cited Siegfried Horn, 'The Old Testament Text in Antiquity', *Ministry*, November 1987, pages 4-8.
[2] Sir Frederic Kenyon, *Our Bible and the Ancient Manuscripts*, fourth edition (1939), page 47.
[3] F. F. Bruce, *The Books and the Parchments*, revised edition (1984), page 107.

Dead Sea discoveries

A fascinating find. When Muhammad ed Dhib, a young bedouin shepherd, lobbed a stone into a hole in the wall of the mountain fronting the Dead Sea he had no idea that the echo would be heard around the world. After all, he was only out looking for a goat gone missing.

What he heard was the shattering of pottery. Wearily the lad pulled himself up the limestone cliffs, still calling the animal as he went. The heat was fierce.

Nearer to the aperture now, he threw a second stone. Again the same sound; the breaking of pottery.

His curiosity heightened, the youth pulled himself up to the hole then peered into the gloom of a small cave. He had only an instant to look. His fingers lost their grip and he fell. But in the brief glimpse he had had into the interior of the cave he had seen enough to fire his courage.

He climbed up a second time. He found a considerable number of cylindrical jars with distinctively shaped caps. Did they contain gold, jewels? Round about were the fragments of the jars his pebbles had broken.

His nose had scented something far more valuable than any goat. Belonging to the Ta'amireh tribe who wandered across the Wilderness of Judaea between Bethlehem and the Dead Sea, he ran with the speed and agility of one of the local ibex to the shade of the hung animal skins, stakes and stench he called home.

He reported his find to an elder of his family. He too was interested and insisted on being taken to the spot. But tomorrow would be soon enough.

The next day found them both cramped in the cave. There were counted seven or eight jars. Some of them were empty. Others were filled with what looked like bundles of rags. They felt they might be on to something when they came across some folds of smooth brown leather.

With their finds they returned to the encampment. Here irreverent hands unrolled a scroll almost 2,000 years old. It stretched from one end of the tent to the other. They were looking at what would become known as the larger of the two Isaiah scrolls.

It was felt that their find had been, after all, quite useless. They could not read the writing. The leather was too fragile to be put to any practical use. For a time, as the bedouins moved from place to place with their goats, they carried the scrolls with them and used them for trade with their neighbours. Some they kept, resolving to take them to Bethlehem. Perhaps there they would fetch a better price.

Market day in Bethlehem found them in earnest barter with a Syrian Christian, by trade a cobbler. He saw little practical value in the scrolls, but thought they might serve as raw materials for his shoe-mending business. Thereafter they were left kicking about the floor of his cobbler's shop for some days.

Then he had a bright idea. The characters on the ancient scrolls looked somehow intriguing. Up at Jerusalem there would be someone who could understand the writing and therefore the value of the scrolls. He took them to the Syrian convent of St. Mark in the Old City. Only then did the cobbler realize that the scrolls had considerable monetary value.

Expeditions were organized to the caves. Soon every cave and cleft of the rock within the vicinity of the original find was being ransacked. Complete secrecy shrouded their operations; they were acting illegally. Under the laws of the British Mandate the authorities should have been informed immediately. Instead the Syrian Metropolitan began to hawk

A fragment of a scroll found in the caves of Qumran. These first-century BC documents represent all Biblical books except Esther.

Part of the complete Isaiah Scroll found at Qumran. Scholars reading the scroll in 1948 found that the Hebrew text on which the modern Bible translations are based had not changed since the time of Christ.

the fragments and the scrolls around the various scholarly institutions in Jerusalem to ascertain their exact worth. It was when he showed them to Professor E. L. Sukenik of the Hebrew University that the reverberations of the original find began to be felt throughout the world.

Dr. John Trever of the American School of Oriental Research was the one who announced that what they were looking at was the scroll of Isaiah in pre-Christian Hebrew inscribed on papyrus. 'You are holding', he told the Metropolitan, 'the oldest manuscript of the Bible ever known.'

The story was out.

The original find had been made in March 1947. Now, almost twelve months later, archaeologists and specialists in ancient languages began to converge on the spot. The manuscripts discovered up to that time were moved to the Archaeological Museum (now known as the Rockefeller Museum), Jerusalem.

There was tremendous excitement in the scholarly world. The excitement soon communicated itself to the world of journalism, and a greater convergence of bodies occurred in Jerusalem. Within a little more than twelve months of the original find the 'Dead Sea scrolls' were making headlines around the world.

Those questions which had been hammering on the door of Judaeo-Christian scholarship for so long were about to be answered.

The main finds were made in caves around Qumran. Soon the caves were numbered, Muhammad ed Dhib's cave being Cave I. Cave IV was a particularly rich one containing 35,000 scroll fragments. Scholars, rather than bedouins, now took the lead in searching for more 'treasure'. Eventually ten manuscript-containing caves were found in the vicinity of Qumran, four in the Wadi Murabba'at near Bethlehem, a small number in a valley south of En-gedi, and a few more during excavations of Masada, where the Zealots had held out against General Silva from AD 70 to 73.

The Essenes

During the period when the Seleucid Kings Antiocus III and Antiocus IV were enforcing the Greek language and culture on Palestine, a community of ultra-pious Jews established themselves at Qumran on the northern shores of the Dead Sea.

They were part of the reaction to the Hellenization process.

While Jerusalem and Judaean Jews revolted under Maccabaean leadership the Essenes were building a monastery (now completely excavated). Behind their monastery was the limestone face of the wilderness of Judaea honeycombed with caves. Their life-style was ascetic and their leader known as the Teacher of Righteousness.

The earliest coins found on the Qumran site date from the reign of John Hyrcanus (134-104 BC), and the most recent coins date from the period AD 132-135, the time of the second Jewish revolt. However, it would appear that the monastery was vacated in AD 70 and that the period of occupation at the time of the second revolt was but a brief one. It is likely that the Essenes fled in AD 70 when they learned of the fall of Jerusalem and the approach of the Roman armies down the Jericho road towards the Dead Sea. Some unquestionably fled to Masada and perished with the Zealots there in AD 73.

Central to the Qumran monastery had been the Scriptorium. Unquestionably an important part of the work of the Essene community was to copy out the Old Testament Scriptures, together with other literature. Among the manuscripts discovered in the caves was *Manual of Discipline* or the *Rule of the Community*. This valuable document gives us an insight into the life and beliefs of the community. They lived, they believed, in an age of unparalleled wickedness. The days of judgement prophesied by Jeremiah and Ezekiel were at hand. They were 'the Elect', 'the Saints of the Most High', 'the Sons of Light': a remnant of the faithful in a perverse generation.

The aim of the Essenes was to study the Scriptures, interpreting them along the lines set down by their Teacher of Righteousness. The Messianic age was about to dawn; then they could look forward to a new temple, a new sacrificial system, and a worthier priesthood. Until the dawn of that age they must devote themselves to strict adherence to the law of God and to the study and reproduction of the sacred writings.

When they learned in AD 70 that General Titus had put Herod's temple to the torch they may have thought that the new age had dawned. If so, the mass slaughter in Galilee under Vespasian and latterly by Titus at Jerusalem, together with the thunderous tread of the legions approaching on the Jericho road must have given them reason for doubt. Their reaction must have been pre-planned, the caves pre-selected, the cylindrical vessels prepared. Whether the Roman slaughter represented an end or a beginning, of one thing the Essenes were determined: they would preserve for posterity the sacred Scriptures which they had — over centuries — so painstakingly set down.

The distribution of the cylindrical vessels containing the scrolls over such a wide area, in the most inaccessible of caves, was in itself a mammoth task. If it did, indeed, take place as the legions thundered down mountain from Jerusalem, it must have been undertaken with speed and great efficiency. Whatever their expectations or their fate it is unlikely in the extreme that the Qumran Essenes expected that their sacred Scriptures would remain undiscovered for 1,877 years.

The Scrolls

Though some discoveries were still to be made, by the end of 1952 the scale of what had been found was apparent.

Biblical scholars were beginning to refer to two eras in biblical studies: BQ and AQ, before Qumran and after Qumran.

In modern Jerusalem, not far from the Knesset, is a strangely shaped building. The visitor has to be informed that this modern building has been designed to resemble the shape of the curious caps from the cylindrically-shaped vessels in which the scrolls had been found. It is called the Shrine of the Book. It has been built as a permanent home for the scrolls where the air is continually controlled and conditioned to facilitate their indefinite preservation. Here the scrolls are on show, including the one perfectly preserved scroll, the famous Isaiah scroll. Others are a little more fragmentary. But the fragments have, in many cases, been pieced together. The oldest manuscripts date from the third century BC. There is a wealth of non-biblical material. But the amount of biblical and biblically-related material is overwhelming. Every Old Testament book is represented with the single exception of the book of Esther.

The most recent 'discovery' was made by Yigael Yadin in Bethlehem during the Six-Day War, 1967. It is the twenty-eight-foot long Temple Scroll. Yadin confiscated it in Bethlehem and, when the war was over, purchased it from its owners for the Shrine of the Book. Its chief value is in the further insights it has provided into the life of the Essene community at Qumran.

Significance of the discoveries

Until 1947 the most ancient Old Testament manuscript was the Masoretic text of AD 900.

Suddenly everything had changed.

The central point of interest for those like W. F. Albright and Siegfried H. Horn who converged on Jerusalem in the early 1950s was to ascertain the extent to which the 2,000-year-old Dead Sea scrolls would uphold the accuracy of the

(Above) Wadi Qumran on the north-western shores of the Dead Sea about nine miles south of Jericho. In the caves in this area a Jewish sect, the Essenes, hid some of their precious scrolls as they fled from the Romans in AD 66-70. Other scrolls were simply left in the caves where they lived. (Below) Inkwells uncovered during the excavations of the ruins of Khirbet Qumran.

Masoretic text and, therefore, the accuracy of the Old Testament accepted by Christians and Jews for so long.

Albright had been among the first to sense the importance of the scrolls. In the spring of 1948 he had told his students that the finds by the Dead Sea represented 'the greatest manuscript discovery of modern times'. In the months and years thereafter he, and many others, spent thousands of hours poring over detailed photographs of the scrolls.

The scrolls were categorized, identified and pieced together. Some scholars were particularly interested in what the non-biblical scrolls could teach them about the Essenes and the century in which they had lived. Others, like Albright, were concerned with the all-important comparison between the Hebrew content of the scrolls and the Hebrew Old Testament based on the Masoretic text of AD 900 (for two centuries dismissed by many experts as a bowdlerized and vastly inaccurate copy of the Scriptures extant at the time of Christ).

More was at stake than the reputation of the Masoretes as copyists. The real issue was the dependability of an important part of the source upon which Christian doctrine was based, the Scriptures revered by Jews and Christians.

By 1952 the careful comparison of the contents of Cave I (dating from the time of Christ) with the Masoretic text (dating from the tenth century) was complete. *The texts were, to all practical purposes, identical.* Differences were almost exclusively spelling mistakes, or of a grammatical nature. At no point did they affect the sense of the biblical text then in use. It appeared that the Hebrew Bible extant in the days of Jesus was the same as the Masoretic text from which the currently used Old Testament had been translated. The Isaiah scroll from Cave I, much abused by the bedouins and the Bethlehem cobbler, contained a text form virtually identical to the printed Hebrew Bibles then in use.

As the years passed and the contents of the other caves were examined and compared much was learned. There had been a few minor omissions and additions, but the Masoretic text reflected the scrolls fairly faithfully. In places the content of the scrolls was closer to the Septuagint (the Greek translation of the Old Testament) than the Masoretic text. This illustrated that the Septuagint translators had followed a Hebrew 'revised version' different from the revision favoured by the Masoretes. But, these minor considerations aside, the message of the Dead Sea scrolls was this: *the text of the Old Testament had been preserved unchanged down the centuries.*

But what of the experts who, since the eighteenth century, had taught that, down the centuries, the biblical text had experienced 'a degree of corruption beyond our wildest imagination'? And what of the thousands who had believed them?

Most were dead. Others embarrassed. Many admitted that, after all, the Masoretic Bible was essentially the same as the Bible of Jesus and the apostles. A few, however, prepared to fight another day. . . .

Controversy over the Scrolls

There was a feeling even among conservative Jewish and Christian scholars that the finds by the Dead Sea were too good to be true. Had they been asked previously they would unquestionably have said that a find on this scale was way beyond the realms of possibility.

Other scholars felt even more strongly that the plethora of scroll discoveries in the region of the Wilderness of Judaea was too good to be true. In the scholarly world rarely, if ever, had an entire school of thought been demolished so totally and so decisively. As the closeness of the Dead Sea manuscripts with the Hebrew Bible was being demonstrated, the highbrow critics shifted the ground of their criticism. They attacked the genuineness of the scrolls.

As each wave of assertion and counter-assertion emerged

from Jerusalem and from the university campuses of Western countries, the controversy was faithfully reported by the world's press. Rarely had the pronouncements of fusty academics made such headlines.

From Europe and the United States the dating of the scrolls — from the third century BC (very largely) to AD 70 — was hotly contested.

But as more scientific explorations took place and more scientific tests were applied the age and genuineness of the scrolls was upheld.

As the Qumran monastery was excavated, the evidence of pottery, coinage and other artifacts attested to the fact that the Essenes had occupied the site throughout the last three centuries before Christ and until AD 70. There was then evidence of a brief Roman occupation of the site. Finally, scholars found artifacts which pointed to a further period of Jewish occupation at the time of the second Jewish revolt of AD 135. Thus the archaeological evidence authenticated the dating of the manuscripts.

There was, in addition, scientific evidence. The linen wrappers containing the scrolls were subjected to carbon-14 dating tests. The great majority of the scrolls were dated in the three centuries before Christ, a few in the century after Christ and a very few in the second century AD (coincident with the occupation of the site during the second Jewish revolt).

Again the critics were silenced. It was agreed that the age and genuineness of the scrolls was beyond dispute.

Sources

Siegfried H. Horn, 'The Old Testament Text in Antiquity', *Ministry*, November 1987, pages 4-8.
Siegfried Horn, *The Spade Confirms the Book* (second edition 1980).
J. A. Thompson, *The Bible and Archaeology* (third edition 1982).
J. M. Allegro, *The Dead Sea Scrolls* (1956).
John Allegro, *The Dead Sea Scrolls: A Reappraisal* (1964).
Edmund Wilson, *The Dead Sea Scrolls: 1947-1969* (1969).
W. H. Brownlee, *The Meaning of the Qumran Scrolls for the Bible* (1964).

6

The battle for the New Testament

The 'Battle for the Old Testament' was won with the aid of a discovery made by a bedouin shepherd. The 'Battle for the New Testament' was won with the aid of a discovery by a German professor.

The bedouin's discovery occurred by accident and was accomplished in seconds. The German's discovery occurred after years of search that served to occupy much of his career.

The German professor's name: Constantin Tischendorf.

Tischendorf's mission

Trained in the theology school of the University of Leipzig, Tischendorf's background did not make him an obvious candidate to be a defender of the New Testament. In the year in which he took his doctorate — 1838 — the conventional wisdom among German theologians was hotly opposed to the reliability of the New Testament. But Tischendorf was prepared to swim against the tide.

His studies led him to the view that the gospels *were* authored, not only by eye witnesses of the events recorded, but by Matthew, Mark, Luke and John specifically, and that the text was entirely to be trusted. While other German theologians asserted that Paul wrote only four of the epistles attributed to him — Romans, 1 and 2 Corinthians and Galatians — Tischendorf's careful examination of language and style led him to the view that Paul had written them all.

Soon he found himself right in the centre of the nineteenth century debate as to whether the New Testament in general was reliable. Edward Gibbon in *The Decline and Fall of the Roman Empire* — written in the previous century — had launched the debate with his assertion that early Christian leaders 'with rash and sacrilegious hands' had tampered with the original New Testament manuscripts. Richard Porson of Cambridge made a crusade out of New Testament criticism.

Heinrich Paulus of Heidelberg and David Strauss of Zurich were soon attacking the whole miraculous content of the New Testament. Perhaps Ernest Renan, a Frenchman, went furthest when he treated the life of Christ as no more than a romantic piece of theatre. Tischendorf's 'work came not a moment too soon'.[1]

It frustrated Tischendorf that biblical critics were able so easily to uncover inaccuracies in vernacular Bibles. He was angry that Bible translators, from Martin Luther to his own century, had used the Greek New Testament of Erasmus (1516) so uncritically. He believed that the work of the Dutch Renaissance scholar was slapdash and deeply flawed. What was needed, he decided, was an accurate text of the New Testament based on the most ancient of manuscripts. He decided to spend his life discovering just such a manuscript. It would, he wrote, confound 'the dazzling wit and ingenious sophistry' of those who 'torture and twist the facts which occurred 1,800 years ago'. 'I am confronted by a sacred task,' wrote Tischendorf to his wife Angelika, 'the struggle to regain the original form of the New Testament'.

First attempt

There were four ancient manuscripts of the New Testament when Tischendorf began his search. The first, the *Codex Alexandrinus*, was 1,300 years old and owned by the British Museum. The second, the *Codex Claramontanus*, was almost as old and owned by the national library of Paris. Both manuscripts were incomplete.

The other two ancient manuscripts were the *Codex Vaticanus* and the *Codex Ephraemi*. The first dated from the middle of the fourth century, was owned by the Vatican and not available to any Protestant scholar. The second was accessible in Paris but unreadable. Its fifth century text of the Bible had been more or less erased a few centuries after it had been written and the writings of Syrian scholar Ephraem inscribed over it.

The difficulties facing Tischendorf in finding a new, definitive edition of the Greek New Testament were formidable!

He accepted them as a challenge.

He would, he said, produce his definitive Greek New Testament within the year!

He went to Paris. Here he abused his eyes by spending months poring over the faded *Codex Claramontanus* and the largely erased *Codex Ephraemi*. With super-human effort he managed to transcribe sixty-four faded Old Testament leaves and 145 largely erased New Testament pages.

At the British Museum, like many before him, he was given unrestricted access to the *Codex Alexandrinus*.

It was in Rome that he was stone-walled. After initially being refused access to the *Codex Vaticanus*, he persisted with his pressure. At last he was permitted just six hours with it.

As promised, his Greek New Testament was ready within the year. But he was dissatisfied. In his heart he knew that it was little better than that produced by Berlin professor Karl Lachmann in 1831. Even the best of the manuscripts to which he had had limited access contained only parts of the New Testament.

He decided: as yet undiscovered manuscripts must be found on which to establish the authentic text of the New Testament.

Rumours from the East

In 1838 American archaeologist Dr. Edward Robinson made one of his celebrated trips to the Middle East. At the same time Tischendorf was committing to paper the belief that 'in some recess of the Greek or Coptic, Syrian or Armenian monasteries, there might be some precious manuscripts slumbering for ages in dust and darkness'. Edward Robinson confirmed his hunch. He reported that in St. Catherine's monastery on Mount Sinai there was a large and untouched library of the most ancient manuscripts imaginable.

Tischendorf was not to know it, but St. Catherine's — for reasons embedded in its unique history and unbeknown to anyone — contained the largest collection of the most ancient biblical manuscripts in the world. And that among them was 'a jewel beyond price'.

St. Catherine's is the oldest continuously inhabited monastery in Christendom. It was founded by order of the Emperor Justinian in AD 527 and named in honour of Catherine, a Christian martyr broken on the wheel in AD 307.

A vast number of monasteries were founded during the Byzantine period. In their early years, like St. Catherine's, they would have sought to accumulate libraries of manuscripts. However, most if not all fell prey to one or other of the waves of invaders which periodically swept across the Middle East.

What preserved the library at St. Catherine's from the sackings in which many of the other monastic libraries perished was the political tradition there. That tradition was a settled policy, not only of political non-alignment, but of actively currying the favour of each successive conqueror. By the nineteenth century all the monks at St. Catherine's were Greek. In earlier centuries there had been a mix of Greeks, Syrians, Georgians and Ethiopians. The multi-national nature of the group helped perpetuate the political flexibility which preserved their library, and them, from destruction.

In AD 625 the monks even sent a delegation to Muhammad himself begging his protection. This was to be the beginning of their uniquely tolerant relationship with Islam. Annually they petitioned Constantinople requesting continued protection. In AD 1115 they petitioned Crusader King Baldwin of Jerusalem *not* to pay them a visit! They wanted above all to avoid alienating the Sultan.

Tischendorf and the Christian world were to have reason for gratitude to the monks whose careful diplomacy had preserved the manuscripts through many centuries of bloodletting and destruction.

On the track

Mount Sinai; a triangle of mountains, a rock barrier between Asia and Africa. From the summit, 2,260 metres above sea level, the view is one of gaunt ridges and cragged peaks exuding the breath of the Old Testament. This moonscape is bluish in the shade, lion-coloured where the sun penetrates, sometimes rippled and sometimes scooped out into whorls.

This is the setting for the monastery of St. Catherine.

In March 1844 Tischendorf took ship from Italy for Alexandria. From Alexandria he made his way to Cairo. Monks representing St. Catherine's were there to meet him. They told him they had priceless manuscripts in the monastery; but something in their tone told Tischendorf they had no idea *how* priceless.

The journey from Cairo to Mount Sinai was a hazardous one. It took twelve days to reach the Plain of Raha from which rises the northern extremity of Mount Sinai.

At the monastery a basket was let down. Tischendorf placed in it a letter of recommendation he had brought with him. The basket was drawn up into the monastery. When it was let down again the monks had attached a crossbar to it. Tischendorf first, then the remainder of his party were drawn up one by one.

The monastery's literary treasures were contained in the narthex. To reach the huge wooden doors of the narthex, Tischendorf and his party had to descend steeply. The church was lower than almost any part of the interior of the monastery walls, and the narthex was a kind of ante-nave.

The narthex or library was, according to Tischendorf, 'a poor place to which no one in the monastery paid much attention'. Nevertheless the appointed librarian Kyrillos was helpful. As Tischendorf discovered the manuscripts one by one in the course of May 1844 Kyrillos extended to him a courtesy that few more professional librarians would have permitted. Tischendorf was allowed to take the priceless manuscripts from the narthex and examine them at his leisure in his own room.

Towards the end of May he felt he had found 'the pearl of all my researches'. 'I perceived in the middle of the great hall a large and wide basket full of old parchments; and the librarian, who was a man of information, told me that two heaps of papers like these, mouldered by time, had been already committed to the flames. What was my surprise to find amid this heap of papers a considerable number of sheets of a copy of the Old Testament in Greek, which seemed to me to be one of the most ancient that I had ever seen.'

Of the 129 parchments he discovered, Kyrillos permitted Tischendorf to take forty-three of them home with him. With these parchments he returned to Cairo.

In 1846 Tischendorf published a brilliant edition of the forty-three parchments under the title *Codex Frederico-Augustanus*. The King of Saxony had paid his expenses; it seemed right to him that his findings should bear the king's name.

The discovery

But Tischendorf had not found that for which he was searching: an ancient and a complete manuscript of the New Testament.

In 1853 he set off again visiting monasteries in Libya, Cairo, Alexandria, Jerusalem, Laodicea, Smyrna and Constantinople, as well as St. Catherine's in Sinai.

At St. Catherine's he asked the monks to produce the eighty-seven parchments he had seen nine years earlier. For reasons best known to themselves they refused to allow him access and, indeed, denied all knowledge of the existence of the parchments. Nevertheless Tischendorf returned with the finds from the other monasteries and was able to publish, based on them, an improved edition of the Greek New Testament.

As the months went by the dusty depths of St. Catherine's occupied Tischendorf's imagination. He felt that there were many treasures there still to be uncovered and that the monks were perhaps deliberately preventing him from having access to them.

Soon a third visit to St. Catherine's was being planned. This time the finance came from the Tsar of Russia. The condition imposed by the Tsar was that any discoveries made by Tischendorf were to become the Tsar's property.

The third visit, at first, promised to be even more disappointing than the second. After several days of foraging among the dust clouds in the narthex of St. Catherine's Tischendorf grew impatient. He told his companions that he would give it another three days and then return to Cairo.

This three-day period proved to be vital. In it he uncovered 346 parchments (all in the same handwriting) — including a codex which contained the whole of both the Old and the New Testaments. It was of incredible age. Tischendorf had uncovered the pearl of great price; achieved the aim of a life-time.

To his wife he wrote: 'It is the only such manuscript in the world. Neither the *Codex Vaticanus* nor the London *Alexandrinus* contains the whole New Testament, and the *Sinai Codex* is undoubtedly older than both. This discovery is a remarkable occurrence and a great one for Christian knowledge.' Tischendorf was in no way exaggerating.

References
[1] James Bentley, *Secrets of Mount Sinai* (1985), page 29.

The find of a lifetime

Tischendorf made his great discovery in the monastery on Mount Sinai in 1859.

The *Codex Sinaiticus* — the complete Old and New Testament in 'book' as opposed to 'scroll' form — was older than the oldest (incomplete) manuscript extant. Tischendorf was sure that it dated from very early in the Christian era. 'I was', he wrote, 'beside myself with joy.'

It is regrettable for his reputation that Tischendorf, at this point, allowed his enthusiasm to get the better of him.

The Russian connection

Remembering his promise to the Tsar — a condition agreed to in haste to secure the finance for this, his third venture — Tischendorf began to make plans to remove the Codex from its home on Sinai. In addition to his promise it is also likely that his reasoning went something like this: Only by removing this priceless manuscript from the place where it had been ignored for so long could the world be given an extraordinary enrichment of Christian knowledge.

Playing for time Tischendorf with others accomplished the time-consuming task of copying out the Codex. At the same time he sought to implant into the minds of the monks the idea of making a presentation of the Codex to the Tsar.

But the minds of the monks had been much altered since his first visit in 1842. Now they were loath to allow any manuscript out of the monastery. The best that Tischendorf could do was to persuade them to make the Codex not a gift but a loan to the Tsar.

With this ruse he wrested the Codex from its home and removed it to St. Petersburg. The monks were never to see their Codex again.

On 19 November 1859, wrote Tischendorf, 'I presented to their Imperial Majesties, in the Winter Palace . . . , my rich collection of Greek, Syriac, Coptic, Arabic and other manuscripts in the middle of which the Sinaiticus Bible shone like a crown.' There was not so much as a whisper that the Sinaiticus Bible was not his to give.

Soon Tischendorf was under pressure from the Tsar and the leaders of the Russian Orthodox Church to publish the *Codex Sinaiticus*. This was a task of immense complexity. Like other very early manuscripts — including the originals on which the actual authors of Scripture would have set down their narratives — the *Codex Sinaiticus* contained no divisions into paragraphs, no spaces between the words and no punctuation. Needless to say, it contained no division into verses or chapters.

Tischendorf tackled the task with a will. In 1862, 223 copies were presented by the Tsar to the great libraries of the world. With no sense of irony whatever the Tsar presented one copy to the monastery on Mount Sinai. Here it remains on display in place of the original. Eventually the monks agreed to sign over their precious manuscript to the Tsar in exchange for a gift of 9,000 roubles and certain political concessions.

But Tischendorf had a tender conscience. The idea that he had 'stolen' the Codex was whispered throughout the scholarly world in which he had many competitors and detractors. The pressure took its toll. Tischendorf suffered stroke after stroke and on 7 December 1874 he died aged 59.

How the Codex came to Britain

The *Codex Sinaiticus* remained in St. Petersburg — renamed Petrograd, then Leningrad — through the Bolshevik Revolution. Financial pressures following the revolution led the leaders of the Soviet Union to offer priceless manuscripts for sale. In 1933 information reached Sir Frederic Kenyon of the British Museum that the Soviet government was planning to sell the *Codex Sinaiticus* for £200,000. He immediately began to canvass support for the project but, in the event, was only able to offer £40,000. The Soviets then reduced their price to £100,000. Sir Frederic felt that this was not an opportunity to be missed. He arranged a consultation with Prime Minister Ramsay McDonald and the Archbishop of Canterbury. Both were soon as excited about the project as Sir Frederic himself. Sir Frederic was given authority to raise his bid to £60,000. But the Russians stuck out for their £100,000.

Immediately prior to Christmas 1933, at the height of the Depression, the National Government put the project of the *Codex Sinaiticus* before the nation. They would guarantee to pay half the price if the British public could come up with the other half.

Collections were made from door to door. Despite massive unemployment and immense privation the required sum of money was raised.

The *Codex Sinaiticus* arrived at the British Museum in a taxi with a *Daily Express* reporter for company.

The significance of the Codex

Tischendorf died in the belief that he had achieved his life's objective. He had provided the world with a witness to the pure, uncorrupted text of the Scriptures, and above all of the New Testament.

In the same year in which the Codex itself was published — 1862 — he published a book expounding the significance of it. With the *Codex Vaticanus*, he maintained (correctly), the *Codex Sinaiticus* was one of the two earliest copies of the whole Greek Bible. Though there was some argument as to the date of the Sinai Bible, all the experts were prepared to accept Tischendorf's view that it was written in the early to mid-fourth century (*circa* AD 300-350).

Since Tischendorf's death the pieces of the jigsaw have been placed together. In AD 331 Emperor Constantine ordered Eusebius of Caesarea to superintend the copying of fifty accurate manuscripts of the Bible. Constantine even specified the type of parchment on which they were to be written. Eusebius was to secure the services of the most professional scribes available.

Eusebius apparently superintended this task, and the fifty copies were produced to the highest possible standard.

It is widely believed that both the Codex Sinaiticus and the Codex Vaticanus were among those fifty copies.

No one knows for certain how the *Codex Sinaiticus* came into the possession of St. Catherine's monastery. It was written centuries before St. Catherine's was founded. It is, however, known that it was once treasured in the library of Caesarea. Tischendorf's first visit to St. Catherine's had yielded forty-three manuscripts; among them had been the notes of a scribe. From these notes we learn that almost all of the manuscripts originated in Caesarea.

Since Caesarea was taken by the Arabs in AD 638 it can be reasonably conjectured that the *Codex Sinaiticus* — among many other manuscripts — was saved and taken by refugees from Caesarea to the remote monastery on Mount Sinai.

Since Tischendorf's discovery of the *Codex Sinaiticus* and the publication of his commentary no serious revision of the Bible has been undertaken without recourse to them.

The English Authorised Version (the King James Bible) was published in 1611 and based on translation work undertaken much earlier by, among others, William Tyndale. The manuscripts from which they had worked had been much more recent than the *Codex Sinaiticus*. Hence it was the concern of many scholars in the late nineteenth century critically to examine the King James Bible with the *Codex Sinaiticus* for reference. Among these scholars were B. F. Westcott and F. J. A. Hort.

What they found was not earth-shattering, but interesting nevertheless. Those who, through the centuries, copied out by hand the books of the New Testament were, it would appear, guilty of a number of minor errors. In English translations of the New Testament undertaken since this time the variations between the texts have been indicated by footnotes, for example, 'not found in older manuscripts'.

The following represents a sample of the major variations:

The second half of Matthew 6:13 (KJV) reads: *'For thine is the kingdom, and the power, and the glory, for ever. Amen.'* This is absent from both the *Codex Vaticanus* and the *Codex Sinaiticus*.

John 8:1-11 (KJV) is the story of the woman taken in adultery. This story is absent from both the *Codex Vaticanus* and the *Codex Sinaiticus*.

Mark 9:43 (second half), 44 present a picture of hell beloved of the hell-fire preachers of bygone centuries; *'the fire that never shall be quenched: where their worm dieth not, and the fire is not quenched'*. This picture of hell, found nowhere else in Scripture, is completely absent from the *Codex Sinaiticus*.

John 4:9 (last part): *'for the Jews have no dealings with the Samaritans'*. This helpful historical comment is not found in the *Codex Sinaiticus*.

John 5:4 (KJV) reads: *'For an angel went down at a certain season into the pool, and troubled the water: whosoever then first after the troubling of the water stepped in was made whole of whatsoever disease he had.'* This rather strange addition to the story of the man at the Pool of Bethesda is absent from the *Codex Sinaiticus*.[1]

Like Tischendorf, Westcott and Hort believed that these

74

minor additions/alterations had either happened accidentally or had occurred when a fragment of commentary from the margin had been incorporated into the text. Occasionally they believed that scribes had misread/misheard words; more rarely had mistranslated them.

In their Introduction to *The New Testament and the Original Greek*, Westcott and Hort wrote: 'It will not be out of place to add here a distinct expression of our belief that even among the numerous unquestionably spurious readings of the New Testament there are no signs of deliberate falsification of the text for dogmatic purposes. . . . Often the additions to the text which are found in later documents but not in the Sinaiticus are merely harmless, and indeed sometimes positively useful additions.'

Edward Gibbon and other eighteenth- and early nineteenth-century scholars had believed that early Christian leaders had 'with sacrilegious hands' made major alterations in the New Testament text. The discoveries of Tischendorf and the careful scholarship of others have uncovered only minor, trivial differences. None, certainly, that have the slightest bearing on Christian belief. Thanks to the *Codex Sinaiticus* we can say with assurance that in the New Testament of our twentieth century Bibles we have to all intents and purposes the gospels, books and letters as set down by their first-century authors.

After discussing the slight variations between the New Testament portion of the *Codex Sinaiticus* and the later manuscripts on which the contemporary Bible was based, Sir Frederic Kenyon, in 1939, stated: 'Our Bible, as we have it today, represents as closely as may be the actual words used by the authors of the sacred books.'[2]

References
[1] Sir Frederic Kenyon, *Our Bible and the Ancient Manuscripts* (1930) gives a detailed account of all the textual variations. See pages 16 *et seq*; Appendix I, pages 247-256.
[2] Ibid, page 18.

Sources
James Bentley, *Secrets of Mount Sinai* (1985).
S. L. Greenslade (ed.), *The Cambridge History of the Bible: the Rest from the Reformation to the Present Day* (1963), volume 3.
Werner Verner Keller, *The Bible as History* (1956).
John Drane, *Introducing the New Testament* (1986).
John Drane, *Jesus and the Four Gospels: An Illustrated Documentary* (1979).
Siegfried Horn, *Records of the Past Illuminate the Bible* (1963 and 1975).
J. B. Phillips, *The Price of Success: An Autobiography* (1984).
Sir Frederic Kenyon, *The Bible and Modern Scholarship* (1949).
Sir Frederic Kenyon, *The Story of the Bible* (1936).
Sir Frederic Kenyon, *Our Bible and the Ancient Manuscripts* (1939).
B. F. Westcott, *A General View of the History of the English Bible* (third edition 1905).

8

The battle won

The battle for the New Testament had been at its fiercest in the mid-nineteenth century.

F. C. Baur of the 'Tubingen School' had declared nearly all the books of the New Testament to be unauthentic. By 'unauthentic' Baur and his followers meant that the New Testament books could not have been written by either the dates or the authors assigned to them. The only exceptions they were prepared to make were for Paul's letters to the Romans, the Corinthians and the Galatians.

But the Dutch school of van Manen went even further. They were prepared to assign Paul's letters to the Romans, the Corinthians and the Galatians, to the *Pseudepigrapha*. In short, their message was: *None* of the New Testament books were written in the first century or by men who had had first-hand knowledge of the life of Jesus.

In England the climax of the sceptical movement was in the work of W. R. Cassels. His book *Supernatural Religion* (1871-77) was a thoroughgoing attack on belief in miracles and on the date, authority and authenticity of the books of the New Testament.[1]

Clearly the discoveries of Constantin Tischendorf represented a grievous blow to the German, Dutch and English schools of criticism. By discovering a hand-written Greek version of the Bible at the Sinai monastery, by uncovering historical evidence which dated it between AD 300 and AD 350 and by linking it with the *Codex Vaticanus* ('under wraps' at the Vatican for many centuries but now proved to be of approximately the same age as the *Codex Sinaiticus*), Tischendorf had put the critics on the defensive. But he had not put them to rout.

'The merest fragment'

The critics lived to fight another day.

There remained, they argued, a significant period between the first century dates assigned to the New Testament books and the period out of which the *Codex Sinaiticus* and the *Codex Vaticanus* had emerged. Conservative Christian scholars were challenged to provide 'the merest fragment' of a manuscript from between the first century, when the New Testament books were assumed to have been written, and the fourth century in the early part of which Sinaiticus and Vaticanus had been written.

This was quite a challenge!

The critics had reason to believe that the challenge could never be met. And conservative biblical scholars feared that the critics were right.

Sinaiticus and Vaticanus dated from the period when the principal material for book production was *vellum*. Vellum was durable and, as had been demonstrated, could survive for many centuries. Both the critics and the conservative biblical scholars knew full well that before the early fourth century the book material in general use in the Graeco-Roman world was *papyrus*. And they knew, equally well, that papyrus was noted for its perishability.

Even the most optimistic of Christian scholars felt that 'the gap' between AD 100 and AD 300 would never be bridged.

But they were wrong.

More treasures on Sinai

In 1891 papyrus documents began to flow from the warm

sands of Egypt to the libraries and museums of Europe and the United States of America.[2]

St. Catherine's had yet more treasures to yield. The monks in their isolated fastness on Sinai had been, to say the least, rather suspicious of the outside world since Tischendorf had removed from them their precious Codex. It took the studied tact and charm of two highly-accomplished Orientalists from Cambridge, Mrs. Lewis and Mrs. Gibson (twin sisters), to thaw through their icy reserve. After many months of research and study the two Orientalists discovered a partially erased copy of the gospels in Syriac. This copy pre-dated all earlier discoveries up to that time and was generally agreed to have been made before AD 200.

Before anyone had had time to analyse the tremendous significance of what the two ladies had discovered on Sinai, Dr. Ezra Abbot called attention to a commentary on the four gospels in Armenian which he had been studying for a decade or more. This commentary, called in Greek *Diatessaron*, dated from a period earlier than AD 170. But its significance did not stop with its early date. It indicated that by AD 170 the gospels of Matthew, Mark, Luke and John were 'held in an undisputed pre-eminence over all other narratives' of the life of Christ. In short: as early as AD 170 the gospels had acquired a sanctity that only great age could have given them.[3]

By now the massed battalions of the critics were falling back on many fronts.

The warm sands of Egypt

The papyrus documents discovered in the warm, preserving sands of Egypt at the turn of the century related to both testaments. There were portions of the book of Genesis and of the Psalms which dated from the fourth century. There was a collection of the sayings of Jesus — most of which were to be found in the gospels — which dated from the third century. There was a considerable portion of the letter to the Hebrews that dated from the third century.[4]

At Dura, on the banks of the Euphrates in 1920, a group of British army officers made an accidental discovery. The archaeologists were brought in. They identified what had been found as a Roman fort and, in the succeeding years, made a complete excavation of it. Evidence was found which enabled them to piece together its history. It had, for example, been taken by the Persians in AD 256. Prior to its fall its walls had been strengthened by the destruction of a quantity of houses, a synagogue and a Christian church. Among the debris was found a number of papyri and vellum manuscripts which had been protected from the damp in a manner similar to those which had survived the centuries in the Egyptian sands. Among these was a fragment of the already-discovered *Diatessaron* — the commentary on the four gospels in Greek — 'written in a hand of the first half of the third century'.[5] As with Dr. Abbot's *Diatessaron*, the scholars were provided with a mosaic of passages from all four gospels. Scholars agreed that this proved that the *Diatessaron* had existed in Greek before AD 150, and that this 'Commentary' on the gospels was likely to have been in circulation well before the date when the sceptics believed that the gospels themselves had been written![6]

Bridging the 'Gap'

The earliest generations of German, Dutch and English critics were long-since dead. The discomfiture of those who had accepted, taught and popularized their viewpoints increased with every new discovery.

But the worst, for them, was yet to come. The conservative Bible students were to have their greatest triumph since the discovery of the *Codex Sinaiticus*. The new discovery has generally been referred to as the *Chester-Beatty Biblical Papyri*. The discovery was made in 1930. The exact story surrounding the find is known only to the locals who made it. The find was made in a Coptic graveyard near the Nile at Aphroditopolis. Like the Dead Sea scrolls, as yet undiscovered in their caves, these papyri were enclosed in a number of earthenware jars. The bulk of the find was acquired by Mr. A. Chester-Beatty, an American collector who lived in England. A small number of fragments were purchased by the University of Michigan. The discovery was first reported in *The Times* of 17 November 1931. The report announced that a large library of biblical papyri had been discovered and that it consisted of portions of twelve manuscripts of which eight contained books of the Old Testament, and three books of the New Testament. All agreed with British Museum curator Sir Frederic Kenyon that the papyri were 'older by a century or more than the oldest manuscripts (other than very small fragments) hitherto known'.

The Chester-Beatty collection included two substantial manuscripts of Genesis, one from the third, the other from the early fourth century. Between them they covered the greater part of the book. There were manuscripts of Numbers and Deuteronomy — dating from the first half of the second century! (That is, between AD 100 and AD 150.) There was a fragmentary manuscript of Isaiah which dated from the third century, a portion of Jeremiah dating from the late second or early third century, and manuscripts of Ezekiel, Daniel and Esther from the same period.

The papyri covering the New Testament books aroused the most interest. One of them had started life as a copy of all four gospels, plus the book of Acts. It had been written in a small hand which scientists trained in deciphering ancient manuscripts agreed in assigning to the first half of the third century. In other words a full century earlier than either

The Sphinx at Giza (below) dating from the reign of King Khafre of the fourth dynasty, c. 2550 BC. Those who sought to uncover the treasures of the East in the late eighteenth century had the most success in Egypt. By the time Nineveh (left) was discovered archaeology was beginning to emerge as a science.

The search for Babylon preoccupied archaeologists for most of the nineteenth century. Major excavations began in 1899. Typical of the artefacts from this massively beautiful city is the characteristic lion to be found in the British Museum. Reconstructions of the Ishtar Gate (below) are to be found at the State Museum in Berlin and on the site of Babylon in Iraq.

Above, the old Hittite capital Hattushash in Turkey, now called Boghazkoy. Below, Hittite soldiers carved in stone. Before A. H. Sayce began 'digging up Hittites all over the place' in 1876 scholars had laughed off this Old Testament power as 'mythical'.

Above, Herod the Great's 'impregnable' city, Masada, overlooking the Dead Sea. Below, Herod's great palace, constructed atop an artificial hill, just south of Bethlehem: Herodion.

Above, the Qumran caves where bedouin shepherd Muhammad Adh-Dhib found the first of
the Dead Sea Scrolls in 1947. Below, ruins of the Qumran monastery where the Essenes copied
out the Hebrew Scriptures between 134BC and AD70.

Above left, one of the distinctive jars in which the scrolls were found. Above right, an example of the scrolls hidden in Judaean caves in the period prior to the Fall of Jerusalem to Titus. They are now kept in the Shrine of the Book (below) designed to resemble the 'caps' of the stone jars.

The entrance to the Gihon Spring and Hezekiah's Tunnel.

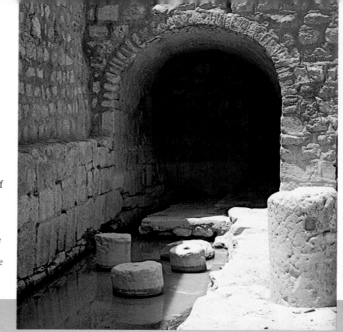

Right, the 1,800-foot Hezekiah's tunnel emerges at the Pool of Siloam. This piece of civil engineering enabled Jerusalem to hold out against the Assyrians. Below, the Hill Ophel. Jebusite walls are visible to the right of the picture.

Sinaiticus or *Vaticanus*. Portions of thirty leaves have been preserved out of the original total of 110. Two contained portions of Matthew's gospel, six of Mark's gospel, seven of Luke's gospel, two of John's gospel, and thirteen of the book of Acts. Sections of Paul's letters to the Romans, Philippians, Colossians and of his first letter to the Thessalonians were found at an earlier stage. Later it was discovered that all of Paul's letters were present in excellent condition. Foremost of papyrologists, Professor V. Wilcken, dated them to about the year AD 200.[7]

The third New Testament manuscript in the Chester-Beatty collection contained a part — approximately one-third — of the book of Revelation. This was dated to the third century.

Light on the Resurrection Puzzle

Meanwhile the significance of an earlier discovery began to be appreciated. Charles Freer of Detroit travelling in Egypt found portions of vellum manuscript which he recognized as being biblical in content. The manuscripts were in the possession of a Cairo dealer. Freer bought them for the United States. They included one of the earliest copies of the gospels in Greek. In addition there were two Old Testament manuscripts covering Deuteronomy and Joshua dating from the fifth or possibly early sixth centuries, plus fragments of the earlier books of Moses, together with the book of Ruth. There was a damaged copy of the Psalms dating from the sixth century. There was another New Testament manuscript including the gospels and the epistles dating from the fourth or fifth centuries. Collectively Freer's finds became known as the *Washington Codex*.

The *Washington Codex* was of interest for more reasons than one. It not only represented another major find in terms of ancient biblical manuscripts. It also helped scholars to understand something that had concerned them since the discovery of the *Codex Sinaiticus*. One of the omissions from the *Codex Sinaiticus* had been the last twelve verses of the gospel of Mark. While containing the Resurrection accounts in detail from the other three gospels, the *Codex Sinaiticus* ends the gospel of Mark with the announcement of the Resurrection, but omits subsequent details, including the commission addressed by the risen Lord to the disciples. Much had been made of this by biblical critics. One peculiar feature of the *Washington Codex* attracted immediate attention from scholars. It contained the disputed last twelve verses from Mark's gospel. This enabled scholars to come to terms with the omission from *Sinaiticus*. *Sinaiticus* omitted the last few verses of Mark, *Vaticanus* omitted the latter part of the letter to the Hebrews. *Both were contained in the Washington Codex.* Many scholars began to put down the omissions to human fallibility or fatigue. Certainly significance ceased to be attached to them.

The Chester-Beatty collection, with the *Washington Codex*, 'between them carried back the textual tradition of the New Testament for a full century . . .' stated Sir Frederic Kenyon in 1948. 'The Chester-Beatty papyri have therefore strengthened very materially the basis — already very strong — of our confidence in the text of the New Testament as it has come down to us.'[8]

The oldest fragment of all

One final dramatic discovery was to be made in the battle for the New Testament. It would appear that the discovery was made as early as 1920, but it was not until 1936 that it was brought to Britain and that experts pronounced on exactly what it was.

The confusion is not too surprising. The oldest of all biblical fragments — now to be found in the John Rylands University Library, Manchester — was simply a torn fragment which for centuries helped to wrap up an Egyptian mummy. Some of the fragments date from the second century *before* Christ and contain verses in Hebrew from Deuteronomy. But the oldest fragment of the *New* Testament, now known as 'the Rylands fragment', dates from the first half of the second century AD. The fragment of papyrus is no bigger than a man's hand and, on both sides, contains verses from the eighteenth chapter of John's gospel (verses 31-33, 37, 38).

The nineteenth-century critics had been unanimous in assigning the gospel of John to a very late date indeed, and in asserting that John's authorship of it was an impossibility. The importance of the Rylands fragment to papyrological experts is that it was written in the first half of the second century, *in other words shortly after John's death (in or around AD 100)*. Hence Christian scholars have reason to be grateful to the Egyptian hands who used this fragment of the gospel to help mummify a body, thus keeping the fragment as well as the body in conditions which would enable both to survive the centuries. The fragment suffices to prove that a manuscript of John's gospel was in circulation in provincial Egypt, where it was found, about the period AD 130-150. Commenting on this Sir Frederic Kenyon states: 'Allowing even a minimum time for the circulation of the work from its place of origin, this would throw back the date of composition so near to the traditional date in the last decade of the first century that there is no longer any reason to question the validity of the tradition.' The tradition being, of course, that John wrote the gospel that bears his name and that he did so in the late 90s of the first century.

In the same year in which the significance of the Rylands fragment was first appreciated, Dr. H. I. Bell and Mr. T. C. Skeat bought three leaves of a papyrus codex for the British Museum. The three leaves contained portions of a life of Christ which, though not drawn from any of the four gospels, do not differ from them. The leaves also contain excerpts from the first three (or synoptic) gospels, and from the fourth gospel. The quotations from John's gospel (5:39, 45; 9:29; 7:30; 10:39) are accepted as further proof of the traditional date of John's gospel and of John's authorship of it. The three leaves of papyrus codex, like the Rylands fragment, are dated in the first half of the second century.[9]

As he reviewed, in 1948, the discovery of biblical manuscripts in the previous half century, Sir Frederic Kenyon believed that the contentions of the mid-nineteenth school of Baur and van Manen had been 'shattered to pieces'.

The time had come, he said, to re-assess the value of the criticism of Scripture which had been characteristic of the previous 150 years with regard to 'the authenticity and authority of the books of which the Bible is composed'. The discoveries of the last half century, and more especially of the last fifteen years, had enhanced the position of the conservative Bible student 'very materially'. It was time 'to shake off the excessive scepticism characteristic of much biblical scholarship in the latter part of the nineteenth century, and to restore confidence in the Bible as a guide to truth and a basis for the conduct of life'.[10]

The higher critics of the nineteenth century had challenged Christian scholars to provide 'the merest fragment' of a manuscript dated from between the first and the fourth centuries. In making their challenge they had been certain that 'the gap' between the time when Christians believed that the New Testament books had been completed (*circa* AD 100) and AD 300-350 (the date of the *Codex Sinaiticus*) would never be bridged.

From the perspective of the mid-twentieth century it appeared that their demand for 'the merest fragment' had been but a modest one. *They had had a veritable avalanche of*

fragments, plus whole libraries of papyri and even more codices.
No one would challenge Kenyon's conclusion: 'A large part
of the gap between the original writers and the earliest manuscripts which we possess has thus been filled.'[11]

Against immense odds and all the probabilities, the battle
for the New Testament had been won. And it had been a rout.

The manuscript evidence for the authenticity of the New
Testament is far, far in excess of that which can be marshalled
for any other document of antiquity. Over 5,300 Greek manuscripts of the New Testament, 8,000 Latin Vulgate and more
than 9,300 manuscripts of other early versions are now available. This contrasts with the next most authenticated work
of ancient times: Homer's *Iliad*. Of Homer's *Iliad* 643 manuscripts survive.

And the variations between the thousands of ancient New
Testament manuscripts? Who better than Professors B. F.
Westcott and F. J. A. Hort, who spent forty years studying
them, to speak on the subject:

'If comparative trivialities such as change of order, the
insertion or omission of the article with proper names, and
the like are set aside, the words in our opinion subject to
doubt can hardly amount to more than a thousandth part of
the New Testament.'[12]

References
[1] Sir Frederic Kenyon, *The Bible and Modern Scholarship* (1948), pages 4-8.
[2] Ibid, pages 16-23; Sir Frederic Kenyon, *The Story of the Bible* (1936), pages 1-110.
[3] Sir Frederic Kenyon, *The Story of the Bible* (1936), page 95.
[4] Sir Frederic Kenyon, *The Bible and Modern Scholarship* (1948), pages 16, 17.
[5] Sir Frederic Kenyon, *The Story of the Bible* (1936), pages 96, 97.
[6] Ibid.
[7] Ibid, pages 113-116.
[8] Sir Frederic Kenyon, *The Bible and Modern Scholarship* (1948), pages 18-21.
[9] Ibid, pages 21-23. Kenyon adduces further compelling evidence for John's authorship of
the gospel that bears his name. See pages 23-26.
[10] Ibid, pages vii, 23.
[11] Sir Frederic Kenyon, *The Story of the Bible* (1936), page 117.
[12] B. F. Westcott and F. J. A. Hort, *The New Testament in the Original Greek* (1911), volume
I page 2.

THE STORY OF THE ENGLISH BIBLE

9

The Bible and the dawn of Christianity

The Empty Tomb

At the cross the disciples had been broken men.

When rumours of Resurrection had begun to spread they had refused to believe them. And had continued to do so until they had seen and heard and touched and eaten with the Risen Lord.

But as they left the Mount of the Ascension and made for Jerusalem it was as if they trod air.

The three crosses had been taken down.

The tomb nearby — no more than a few hundred yards from the temple precincts — was empty for all to see. If the tomb had *not* been empty, the Jerusalem Establishment could, in a matter of minutes, have disproved the Resurrection. Caiaphas and his priestly conclave could simply have marched down to the tomb, broken the seals and publicly exhibited the mortal remains for all to see. Why had hard-bitten Roman soldiers suddenly deserted their posts and dashed back to face what might have been a court-martial and execution — if there had been no Resurrection? Or why had they been bribed to spread a transparently spurious story when the simplest solution would have been to have marched them back, under escort, proved them wrong, and had them beheaded on the spot as a warning to anyone else who might have fancy, supernatural ideas?

'Had I been Caiaphas and *found* an empty tomb', Mary

Essberger has written, 'I'd have produced a "body" — *any* body — rather than let them get away with it and cause more havoc. That is, unless I, too, was suffering from some psychological shock amounting to a form of mental paralysis. That they did not do this is in itself something of a psychological phenomenon which needs as much investigating as the Resurrection itself. Men of that religio-political calibre would be prevented from such a "cover up" only by some inner uncertainty and confusion, some form of shock and paralysis stemming from a real, though unvoiced fear, or else by the fact that too many people, even among their own number, had seen the empty tomb to make it safe to play any tricks.'[1]

And what about the transformation of the disciples? Wishful thinking? Hardly. Peter had left the tomb 'wondering to himself what had happened'. The others 'did not understand from Scripture that Jesus had to rise from the dead'. 'They did not believe the women (who first brought the news of the Resurrection), because their words seemed to them like nonsense.' Even after the final appearance of Jesus 'some doubted'. Eventually Jesus himself had 'rebuked them for their lack of faith and their stubborn refusal to believe'.[2]

There is no picture here of imagination gone wild, creating a glowing picture of victory to satisfy pious hopes. To sceptical moods, exalted visions do not come. Nor do men seeking to deceive others confess to sadness, despair, fear, unbelief, astonishment.[3]

Evidence, and no doubt?

When, at the Feast of Pentecost, the previously timid band of disciples preached the Good News about Jesus, they did so within yards of what was, at once, the most telling argument and the most striking visual aid for what they preached: the empty tomb. Jesus of Nazareth, they said, represented the culmination in person of every Messianic prophecy of the Old Testament. He was the Christ expected, prophesied for millennia, the hope of all ages past and yet to be.

Soon this small band of followers swelled. Thousands embraced their gospel in a day. And, as the forest fire spread, it made incursions into the Jewish Establishment itself; many priests were converted.[4] There was, apparently, evidence and no doubt.

Most remarkable of all: The hard-headed, flint-hearted, sword-wielding Pharisee with the self-appointed task of smashing the new movement by force, joined it. Joined it, and became its foremost missionary, braving every kind of danger, standing tall against every refinement of persecution. Paul was arguably their finest preacher; certainly their greatest theologian.

Twenty years on Paul was writing to the church he had founded in Corinth. The point has already been made that in the ancient world 'Corinthian' was a by-word for every kind of debauchery and extortion. Paul listed some of the more obvious types in the city: adulterers, perverts, homosexuals, rapists, thieves, swindlers, drunkards. Then he rounded on the Corinthian church and added: *'And such were some of you! But you have cleansed yourselves from all that, you have been made whole in spirit, you have been justified in the name of the Lord Jesus.'*[5]

Not even the most purblind of critics now doubts the authenticity of this letter to the Corinthians, written so soon after the Resurrection and ten years before the first of the four gospels was committed to paper.[6] But has it been overlooked as a proof of the Resurrection? *'And such were some of you.'* What had changed these men and women who lived in the ancient world's sink of iniquity? Paul's charisma? Far from it; the two surviving letters to Corinth demonstrate conclusively that, even among converts, Paul was not universally admired. Paul was quite clear on what had worked the miracle; it was the pardon made available by the death of Jesus and the power made available by his Resurrection. In far-off Corinth they believed it and plugged in to the miracle.

In the same letter written well before the first gospel and, therefore, nearer in time to the Resurrection, Paul lists those who saw Jesus alive after his very public death. Concluding the list he said that 'over 500 Christians' saw Jesus after the Resurrection 'of whom', he says, 'the majority are still alive' and hence available for interview.[7]

An impossible achievement

The ascending Jesus had commissioned his followers to preach his Gospel to every person in every nation. It would have been pardonable to have questioned the judgement of anyone giving such a commission to that particular group of foot-in-mouth faint-hearts. Yet, in metaphors employed at the time, they 'turned the world upside down' and 'set it on fire'. An impossible achievement unless they had, one, an absolute belief in the Resurrection; and, two, had experienced the great supernatural power of the Holy Spirit that Jesus had promised them.

This motley group — most of them uneducated provincials who previously had never stepped outside a land about the size of Wales — took the Good News of Jesus Christ to the limits of the then known world, Roman roads speeding their journey. The almost universal use of the *koine* made communication significantly easier.

Into every district where they went they carried with them an unshakable faith in the fact of the Resurrection, the earth-shuddering power of what they called the 'Holy Spirit' and, equally essential, the Old Testament Scriptures from which to demonstrate that all had been foretold. The substance of the sermons recorded in the Book of Acts and of the theological arguments adduced by Paul, Peter, James and John in their letters to prove the validity of the claims of Jesus, was Old Testament Scripture. Every broad acre and tiny fleck of messianic prophecy had been fulfilled in the life of Jesus. Matthew's gospel was to be a singular demonstration of this.

Among Christianity's first frontiersmen: translators

The first frontiersmen of Christianity pressed further and further. As they did so they discovered that the Hebrew Scriptures which had served as their evangelistic text with the Jews, and the Scriptures in Greek which had enabled them to touch base with both Jews and gentiles, were ceasing to be adequate. They were encountering groups capable of understanding neither language.

Paul's letters, then those of Peter and James, then the gospels, then John's Revelation and, eventually, the letters of John and Jude came to be viewed as valuable and sacred. When this happened the same problem occurred. As the frontiers of Christianity sped back groups were discovered for whom the *koine* of what would become known as the New Testament was either foreign or inadequately understood.

Hence, perhaps by the end of the first century, certainly in the second century, the translation of the Scriptures — both testaments — followed immediately on the introduction of Christianity to a nation with a new language. When the Gospel spread east a Syriac New Testament was one of the first monuments to its power. When it spread west, a Latin translation. Ulfilas, the second bishop of the Goths, gave them the Scriptures in their own language. Miesrob, who framed the Armenian alphabet, also translated the Armenian Bible. [8]

The New Testament was translated into Syriac and Latin by about AD 150 and into Egyptian by about AD 200. Papyri of these early translations are extant. They are copies directly descended from those original translations. As language scholars scrutinize the Syrian, Egyptian and Latin texts they discover the exact Greek text which the translator was working from. Hence it is possible to know, from the Syriac, Latin and Egyptian translations, what words were found in a Greek manuscript which had been extant between AD 100 and 150. This has been another, independent line, along which it has been possible to recover the original texts of our Bible.[9]

The Syrian version has opened up even more exciting lines of enquiry. Syriac was not just the language of Mesopotamia and Syria but, with variations in dialect, one of the everyday languages of Palestine in the days of Jesus. The Syriac translation from the Greek was undertaken by Tatian (born *circa* 110; died *circa* 165). Such a large proportion of Tatian's Syriac Bible was discovered in the Vatican library that it was possible, in 1888, to publish it. This has led scholars excitingly close, not only to the Greek texts of the Gospels at the time, but to the direct speech of the first three-and-a-half decades of the Christian Era.[10]

The Vulgate

The importance of Rome, the arrival of Christianity there, and the spread of Christianity in countries conquered by Rome, made the Latin Bible one of vital importance. The first translation is referred to as 'the Old Latin'. But this was to be superseded by Jerome's Latin Vulgate following Constantine's Christianization of the Roman Empire.

'The Old Latin' translation, made around AD 150, is valuable evidence — perhaps *the* most valuable evidence — of the condition of the New Testament 'in the earliest times'.[11] It is seen by scholars as the last link in the chain from our modern New Testaments to the quill pens of the apostles who wrote the New Testament's original twenty-seven books.

It was in its Latin form that the Bible arrived in the British

Isles. The British Isles were to produce, however, their own breed of champions of the Christ, the cross and the empty tomb. And these champions, so distant from the home of Latin, were to adapt biblical precepts in their own way and teach them in the vernaculars of the rough-and-tumble races of these distant isles. Nevertheless, it would take a thousand years of conquest and internal strife before the southern portion of these isles we call Britain would produce a complete written Bible in the language then spoken by the mass of the people.

References
[1] *Church Times*, Easter 1967, pages 87, 88.
[2] Luke 24:11, 12; John 20:9; Matthew 28:17; Mark 16:14. All quotations from the New International Version.
[3] R. E. O. White, *The Stranger of Galilee* (1978), page 158. See also Frank Morison, *Who Moved the Stone?* (1930).
[4] Acts 6:7.
[5] 1 Corinthians 6:10, 11, Phillips.
[6] J. B. Phillips, *Ring of Truth* (1967), pages 21, 22.
[7] 1 Corinthians 15, Phillips.
[8] B. F. Westcott, *A General View of the History of the English Bible* (third edition, 1905), page 3.
[9] Sir Frederic Kenyon, *Our Bible and the Ancient Manuscripts* (1939), page 155.
[10] Ibid, pages 156-159.
[11] Ibid, pages 170, 171.

Britain's first Bibles

We do not know exactly when the Bible came to Britain or who brought it. We do not know *exactly* when Christianity arrived; except that it was long before Augustine put ashore off Kent in AD 597.

Bede (*circa* 672-735) believed that, during the persecution associated with the name of the Emperor Diocletian (284-305), 'faithful Christians' in Britain 'had taken refuge in woods, deserted places and caves', and that, thereafter, they emerged to rebuild their places of worship and recommence the festivals of the church.[1] Gildas, another historian of the Britons, affirms that at the time of Diocletian's onslaught on the Bible, when the inscription '*Extincto nomine Christianorum*' (the name of Christianity has been destroyed) was put over the ashes of a codex of the Bible, 'parts of the Scriptures were burnt in the streets of British towns'.[2]

Certainly three representatives from Britain attended the Council of Arles in 314. By then Constantine reigned and Christianity was a favoured religion. As previously stated, in 332 the Emperor commissioned from Bishop Eusebius of Caesarea fifty copies of the Scriptures (two of which may well be extant in the *Codex Sinaiticus* and the *Codex Vaticanus*).

The Bible from Bethlehem

But these were Greek Bibles, and Britain's first Bibles were Latin. To be exact: 'Old Latin'. In 382 Pope Damasus commissioned Jerome (*circa* 347-420) to produce a more accurate, authoritative Latin Bible. Jerome had studied Greek and Hebrew, but was by instinct a conservative. Hence the New

Testament he set down was merely a revision of the existing Latin translation. There is some evidence that he had recourse to the Greek manuscripts, but alterations were made only when they were strictly necessary. By contrast his Old Testament was 'an altogether new translation from the Hebrew'.[3] His work was completed about 404, had taken twenty years and had been accomplished in Bethlehem. Jerome worked in one of the complex of caves over which Constantine had built the Church of the Nativity. The neighbouring cave is the one labelled by tradition as the birth place of Jesus. Today Jerome's statue — the inscription calls him Hieronymus — dominates a sun-drenched, palm-lined quadrangle.

Jerome's Bible became known as the *Vulgate*. For a thousand years it was the adopted Bible of Western Christendom. Syrians, Egyptians, Armenians and Persians had their own vernacular Bibles. But Western Europe was content with one Bible in an international language. No great library was without a manuscript. It was copied innumerable times and hence there were innumerable tiny variations from one manuscript to the next. Eight thousand manuscripts are still extant. During the Vulgate's thousand year reign, all books were written in Latin. Latin was the language of the monasteries, the monasteries were the chief centres of learning and all educated men spoke Latin.

The Celtic Church

But if a Latin speaker could be equally at home in Italy, Gaul or southern Britain, there were fringes — Ireland and northern Britain — where Latin culture was not at home, and Christianity developed a different coloration.

The century before Augustine landed in Kent was a glorious period in the history of the Irish church. This was thanks largely to Patrick. Having embraced Christianity in Gaul, he took ship to Ireland and began to evangelize the land where he had once been a slave. There had been Christians in Ireland before him, but Christ had never had a champion there of his calibre.

Patrick's preaching came to the notice of the first of the 'High-Kings' of Ireland. Soon the King's son, Conall, was baptized by Patrick. Thousands followed his lead. Conall's great-grandson Columba was to be the missionary of the Celtic Church to the mainland. With a strong claim through his mother Eithne, it is likely that Columba gave up a throne for the banner of Christ. With twelve friends Columba crossed the Irish Channel in coracles of wicker and hide to take the Gospel to Britain. They landed on Iona, separated by a narrow channel from Mull. Iona became Columba's missionary base, the headquarters of the Celtic Church.

Missionaries from Ireland

Soon Columba and the original twelve were joined by scores, perhaps hundreds of missionaries from Ireland. Landing in the mainland bay which still bears his name, Columba and his missionaries began their work of conversion among the Picts. For two centuries Iona was the nursery of bishops, the centre of education and religious knowledge, and a major ecclesiastical focus for the British Isles.

News of 'the schismatic Celts' reached Rome. The Pope originated the plan to send Augustine to 'correct the obstinate' Celtic Christians. Their 'obstinacy' was largely in their deviant beliefs. Columba and his successor, Aidan, shocked the Papacy by their very devotion to the Latin Bible. The Bible was, they said, the only foundation of belief.

The Celtic Church's view of the primacy of Scripture led them away from the Latin Church in terms of both belief and practice. Finding the idea of an ever-burning hell unbiblical, Celtic Christians identified this idea with heathenism and rejected it. For the Celtic Church — as for the Protestant

Churches which followed the Reformation centuries later —
man was saved 'not by the merits of his deeds', but by the
unmerited favour of Jesus Christ. Among the Celts there was
no hint of a belief in an intermediary priesthood; a man
approached God for pardon directly — on his knees. [4]

By the time Columba died — in the year that Augustine
arrived in Kent — he had founded 300 churches throughout
Scotland. Among the Saxons south of the Thames, Augustine
encountered considerable resistance in his attempts to impose
the Roman order; he had the same experience with the Saxon
kingdoms south of the Humber. [5] But this resistance was
minimal by comparison with that encountered within the
Northumbrian kingdom north of the Humber. [6] Here the
ecclesiastical centre was Lindisfarne, a 'holy isle' placed pre-
cariously between the fury of the North Sea and the bleak,
squally Northumbrian coast. At low tide it was joined by an
uneven causeway to the mainland.

Lindisfarne's Bishop was Aidan, a disciple of Columba, who
had been invited to evangelize Northumbria by the Northumbrian King Oswald. According to Bede, Aidan was 'a man
of outstanding gentleness, holiness and moderation'. [7]

The confrontation between the Celtic Church and the ec-
clesiasticism introduced by Augustine took place at the Council
of Whitby in 664. The Celtic Church was represented by one
of Aidan's successors, Colman, described by Bede as 'another
Irishman' committed to 'Scots teaching'. The Roman model
triumphed, King Oswy accepting the submission by Wilfred
(who represented the Roman cause) that Christ had given the
keys of the kingdom to St. Peter, not to St. Columba.

'The Scots Bishop Colman left Britain,' reports Bede, 'taking
with him the Scots he had collected at Lindisfarne, together
with about thirty English whom he had likewise trained in
the monastic life.' [8] They found another retreat off the coast
of Ireland.

Some have viewed the decision taken at the Council of Whitby as a setback for the Bible and for Bible-based Christianity.

The Lindisfarne Gospels

But Lindisfarne and the Church it represented had carved for itself an abiding place in the history of the English Bible. It was during the halcyon age on Lindisfarne that the famous Lindisfarne gospels were produced. These superbly illuminated manuscripts, now in the British Museum, are the finest artefacts still remaining of the Celtic Church: the tangible bequest of that ancient form of Christianity which had taken such a hold in Ireland, Scotland and Northumbria.

The special feature of the Lindisfarne gospels was the extraordinarily intricate system of interlacing patterns, sometimes geometric and sometimes including animal forms, combined and continued with marvellous precision. These illuminated manuscripts were produced in honour of St. Cuthbert who died in 687. 'The main text is that of the Latin Vulgate; but between the lines a later hand has written a paraphrase of the Latin into the primitive English which we commonly call Anglo-Saxon.'[9]

During the two centuries before the Council of Whitby and the two centuries after, Britain was a melting-pot. Having done their best to teach the Britons how to fight the Picts and Scots, the Romans had left the British Isles. In the age after their departure the Saxons, Angles and Jutes invaded, conquered and, by so doing, poured in another rich mixture of ingredients. This was the land of which Augustine and his successors were ecclesiastical primates.

Caedmon of Whitby

A further significant development in the history of the English Bible was to take place at Whitby. A barrier of language separated the peoples of Britain from the Latin Vulgate of Jerome. The first effort to break it down was made by Caedmon in the cloisters of Whitby Abbey just five years after the famous Council.

The abbey at Whitby reared its high walls on the cliffs turned to the North Sea and all its fury. Below it, where the River Esk found its way to the sea were the hovels of Whitby's inhabitants who eked out a meagre existence from fishing. Caedmon had come to the abbey from the agricultural lands beyond the settlement and, in the words of Bede, was 'well advanced in years' at the time of his arrival. [10]

It would appear that Caedmon discovered his gift for poetry and music quite by accident. At a social gathering it was customary for each guest to be invited to sing to the company. Over long years Caedmon, 'when he saw the harp coming his way . . . would get up from the table and go home'. After one such event, and in the isolation of his home, Caedmon thought he heard a voice calling him to 'sing about the creation of all things'. Thereafter he acquired the ability to sing and compose verses in Anglo-Saxon. He humbly reported to the authorities at Whitby's abbey that he had received this new gift. 'All of them agreed that Caedmon's gift had been given him by our Lord. And they explained to him a passage of scriptural history or doctrine and asked him to render it into verse if he could. He promised to do this, and returned next morning with excellent verses as they had ordered him,' reports Bede. Thus Caedmon became the humblest of the Abbey's lay brothers.

'He sang of the creation of the world, the origin of the human race, and the whole story of Genesis. He sang of Israel's exodus from Egypt, the entry into the Promised Land, and many other events of scriptural history. He sang of the Lord's incarnation, passion, resurrection, and ascension into heaven, the coming of the Holy Spirit, and the teaching of the apostles.' [11]

The important thing was that he did all this in Anglo-Saxon, the language of the common people. Not in Latin, the language of the learned. Caedmon had made the first known attempt at a paraphrase of the Bible — actually, the Bible's best-known stories — in the vernacular.

The 229-page Caedmon manuscript is still to be found in the Bodleian Library, Oxford. Critical examination of the manuscript has brought to light evidence of vigorous editing. Nevertheless, there can be no doubt that the original work was that of the eloquent cowherd who turned up at Whitby Abbey one bright morning, announced his God-given gift and was admitted by Abbess Hilda. This was in 670. He died in the Abbey precincts just ten years later.

Aldhelm — the First Translator

Less romantic, but more significant is the achievement of Aldhelm, Bishop of Sherborn, who died in 709. While Caedmon's achievement is likely to have had more popular impact in his own and in later generations, Aldhelm holds the honour of having been the first translator of a part of the Bible into the native tongue of England. A manuscript of the Psalms in Anglo-Saxon has been preserved in Paris. This may well be Aldhelm's work. [12]

The memory of Lindisfarne, once the nerve centre of Christian endeavour in northern England, was receding into the mists of history. The religious centre which had once contested the spiritual leadership of the West with Rome was forgotten. A new order had taken its place. Under this new order the decrees came from Rome. Northumbria itself had ceased to exist as a separate political entity. But, for all that, the influence and example of Columba, Aidan and the multitude of Scots who had won the North from paganism was not altogether dead.

Caedmon had unlocked some of the Bible's fascination for

the humble mind. Seven years before his death one of his countrymen was born who would continue and extend the work he had begun.

Bede and the Bible

Bede was born in 674 near the monastery at Wearmouth. At the age of 6 he entered the monastery itself. There, as the years passed, he developed into a scholar of lasting renown. He studied Latin, Greek, Hebrew, astronomy, medicine, theology and developed a taste for history.

However, as the years passed, by his own admission, his real enthusiasm was 'to devote myself entirely to the study of the Scriptures'.

At some point in his teen years the orphan Bede entered the new monastery built at Jarrow. At 19 he was appointed a deacon, the first step on the ecclesiastical ladder. More importantly he began writing. Bede wrote verse, history and theology. Without his *History of the English Church and People* we would know little of 700 years of our country's history. It was, of course, written in Latin, as were his commentaries on many books of the Bible.

But Bede was more than a scholar. He had inherited the vision 'that the Scriptures might be faithfully delivered to the common people in their own tongue'. [13] First he translated what he considered to be the essentials of the Christian faith; the Creed and the Lord's Prayer. Then, towards the end of his life, he embarked upon a translation of the gospel of John. He completed the translation on his death bed. During his closing hours he dictated steadily on, his amanuensis Wilbert scribbling anxiously.

'There remains but one sentence', Wilbert said finally. Bede translated from Latin to Anglo-Saxon — the poignant words: 'And there are also many other things which Jesus did, the which, if they should be written every one, I suppose that

even the world itself could not contain the books that should
be written.'

King Alfred the Translator

The fourth link in the chain — Caedmon, Aldhelm and Bede
— takes us by surprise: King Alfred the Great.

Alfred became King of Wessex at 22 in AD 865, and ruled
the kingdom until his death at the age of 50. Much of his
reign was spent in the task of containing the Danish invasion.

But Alfred was a scholar. Aware that the Emperor
Charlemagne had instigated a revision of the Vulgate in the
early ninth century (a task ignored by the church itself until
the sixteenth century), Alfred turned his attention towards
translating parts of the Vulgate into the common tongue. While
Vikings burned their way across England leaving the great
libraries and monasteries in ashes, Alfred was working on a
new system of law. He prefixed this with a translation of the
ten commandments and other extracts from the law of Moses.
In addition he 'translated or caused to be translated, several
other parts of the Bible'.[14] Like Bede, he was engaged in
translation at the time of his death; in Alfred's case it was
the book of Psalms.

An age of change and disorder

In the century and a half before the Norman Conquest of
1066 there was a marked decline in the level of scholarship
among the priesthood. Not only were the common people unable to understand the Latin of the Vulgate Bible, a major
proportion of the clergy did not understand it either.

This accounts for the appearance of *glosses* in this period.
Glosses were word-for-word translations into early English
written between the lines of Latin manuscripts. The first
known example was the Lindisfarne gospel. But glosses did
not become extremely common until the tenth century. Glosses

of the gospels dating from around 950 are to be found in Oxford and at the British Museum. They must have been of considerable value to priests when instructing their congregations.

Work on glosses led, naturally, to a renewed interest in producing an actual translation, independent of the Latin text. A complete English translation of the gospels appeared in the tenth century, apparently for public use. Six copies are extant. The earliest — in the library of Corpus Christi College, Cambridge — was the work of Elfric of Bath and has been dated around AD 1000. There is evidence that a large part of the Old Testament was translated by someone else at about the same time.[15]

The Norman Conquest effectively halted the literary development of the English people for three centuries. The Anglo-Saxon gospels dropped out of use. The common people's access to much of the Bible was provided by crude, rhyming paraphrases.

But the fourteenth century brought with it great changes.

There was the Black Death of 1348-9 in which one-third of the population died. The same period, 1344-50 brought famine and war. Developments like these predisposed men to interpret events in prophetic and millenarian terms.

Similar upheavals in France led to the *Jacquerie* of 1358 — and a preoccupation with matters apocalyptic. It was 'back to the Bible' time. The French first produced a revised edition of the Vulgate, *then the first complete version of the Bible in French.*

The power of the Papacy was in decline. At the height of the Great Schism *three* popes — one in Rome, one in Pisa, one in Avignon — vied for power.

Corruption permeated outward to the higher clergy. The

church became a subject for satire and vilification in England. Corruption and decline reached the monasteries.

Corruption in the church was paralleled by restlessness among the masses. English culture was reasserted. The movement began which led to the work of Langland and Chaucer.

There was a dim awareness that Christendom was being menaced to the East and South by the forces of Islam.

In England 'men turned with intense longing to the Bible'. [16]

A corrupt church. Society in turmoil. The dimly understood menace to Christendom itself. The background was in place against which John Wyclif made his great contribution to the history of the English Bible and of the English church.

References
[1] Bede, *A History of the English Church and People* (Penguin Classics), page 48.
[2] Cited Charles Gulston, *No Greater Heritage* (1960), page 17.
[3] Sir Frederic Kenyon, *Our Bible and the Ancient Manuscripts* (1939), page 174.
[4] Bede, *op cit*, pages 146-148. The beliefs of the Celtic Church are discussed in detail by Leslie Hardinge in *The Celtic Church in Britain* (SPCK, 1972). This book represents a distillation of Dr. Hardinge's PhD thesis (University of London).
[5] Bede, *op cit*, pages 68-107.
[6] Ibid, page 107.
[7] Ibid, page 144.
[8] Ibid, pages 185-192, 193, 213; Sir Frederic Kenyon, *op cit*, page 183.
[9] Kenyon, *op cit*, page 184.
[10] Bede, *op cit*, page 251.
[11] Ibid, page 252.
[12] Kenyon, *op cit*, page 195; B. F. Westcott, *A General View of the History of the English Bible* (third edition 1905), page 4.
[13] Kenyon, *op cit*, page 195; Charles Gulston, *op cit*, pages 35-40.
[14] Kenyon, *op cit*, page 196; Westcott, *op cit*, page 5.
[15] Kenyon, *op cit*, pages 197-199; Westcott, *op cit*, page 6; Gulston, *op cit*, pages 53-72.
[16] Westcott *op cit*, page 11.

11

The Bible for the people

In a bleak churchyard in Lutterworth, Leicestershire, the freezing fog had lifted in late morning. Now an icy wind was beginning to howl through the branches of the leafless trees, bringing with it squalls of sleet.

It was a dark, cold day at the dawn of 1385. A small group of figures, some in cassocks of black or russet, and others with threadbare shawls pulled tightly around their bent shoulders, huddled together over an open grave. There was a flurry of words in Latin as the coffin was lowered. John Wyclif was safe at last from his enemies.

Wyclif had died on the last day of 1384. A few years after the icy day of his burial rude hands were to unearth his coffin, burn its contents and, at the orders of the Bishop of Lincoln, scatter his ashes into the River Swift.

The making of Wyclif

Wyclif's twin crimes had been to expose the corruption of the church of his day and, with a group of scholars, to translate Jerome's 1,000-year-old Latin Bible into English.

John of Wyclif had been born in the village of Wyclif around 1320. The village, like the nearby town of Barnard Castle, clings to the banks of the River Tees. He was the son of the lord of the manor.

The evidence indicates that John left his home village at 14. His older brother was content to remain as parish priest and to preside over the odd, flat-roofed church with its ancient font, stained glass windows and curious arrangement of bells.

His father's manor house was immediately adjacent to the church.

Clearly there was something about John that marked him out from an early age. He was to stand tall among those other North Country heroes of the English Bible — Caedmon, Bede, Cuthbert and Aidan — a legatee, whether he knew it or not, of the Celtic Church and its simple, Bible-based doctrines.

John Wyclif became an undergraduate at Balliol College, Oxford and, much later, was to be elected Master of his college. In these early years he distinguished himself as a scholar and made some prominent friends, among them John of Gaunt, the King's son. There is a record of his having been appointed chaplain to the King and of his having had the degree of Doctor of Divinity conferred upon him.

For the future, however, his friendship with John of Gaunt who exercised feudal dominion over the northlands was to prove a matter of life and death to him. John of Gaunt was based in the castle at Richmond, not far from the place of Wyclif's birth. But his power extended as far south as the villages of Fillingham, Lincolnshire, and Lutterworth, Leicestershire, where Wyclif was to be priest, as well as to Oxford where, in practice, he was to spend the greater part of his working life.

Wyclif's only excursion outside of his own country, in 1374, was to be in company with John of Gaunt. Both men visited Bruges in Flanders. John of Gaunt was there to negotiate peace with the French. John of Wyclif was part of an investigative commission appointed by Parliament to enquire into the number of ecclesiastical benefices in England held by foreigners. Wyclif's disillusionment with the church and the Papacy dates from his visit to Bruges. From Bruges he emerged a reformer. His reforming zeal was to gain in intensity as the Papal Schism scandalized even the most devout. Soon he would be a marked man and the target of papal bulls. Only John of Gaunt's intervention and the current weakness of the Papacy enabled him to die peaceably.

Though spending the greater part of his time at Oxford until the spring of 1381, Wyclif was appointed to the living at Fillingham in 1361. It was there in his preaching that the influence over him of Thomas Bradwardine of Merton College, Oxford became apparent. The 'Profound Doctor', apparently, espoused a particularly extreme version of the doctrine of predestination. Wyclif himself preached that no man could know whether he was numbered among the 'elect' and that Christ was, in effect, 'the redeemer of only a fraction of mankind'.[1] This grisly creed, however, did not seem to damage his effectiveness either as priest or academic.

It was at Fillingham that his feud with the mendicant friars began. The mendicants, who had set out to reform the monastic system, had by this time become more corrupt than the system they had set out to change. It is likely that it was from his battle with the mendicants that Wyclif conceived of the idea of translating the Bible so as to reveal to his parishioners the fraud and greed of the mendicants and the system they represented.

Public Controversies

Wyclif's middle life was marked by his involvement in public controversies. The massive financial cost of the protracted wars with France, the demands for money from the Papacy, and the ostentatious wealth of the high dignitaries of the church who supported Papal claims, shuddered discontent through English society. Wyclif's treatises and sermons against these disorders did not, in themselves, mark him out as a front-rank reformer. What *did* make him stand out were his aristocratic connections and the fact that Oxford afforded him a great many public platforms from which to preach. His influence was such that, by 1371, he was in the forefront of religious and

Here ben writun the names of alle the Bookis that ben in this newe Testament, and on every Bookis name the noumbre of the Chapitris ben writun also.

The foure Evangelists	Seynt matheu Seynt mark Seynt luk Seynt Joon	with	xxviii. xvi. xxiv. xxi.
The ten pistlis that Seynt Poul wroot to dyuerse chirchis : & foure that he wroot to certeyne persones.	to Romayns the first to Corinthis the secounde to Corinthis to Galathies to Effecies to Philipensis to Colocensis (to Laodicensis) the firste to Tessalonicensis the secunde to Tessalonicensis the firste to Thimothie the secunde to Thimothie to Tite to Filemon to Ebrews	with	xvi. xvi. xiii. vi. vi. iiii. iiii. i. chapitris. v. iii. vi. iv. iii. i. xiii.
The pistle of Luk Actus of Apostlis		with	xxviii.
The sevene pistlis of Christen feith.	of James the firste of Petre the secunde of Petre the first of Joon the secunde of Joon the thirdde of Joon And of Judas	with	v. v. iii. v. i. i. ii.
the Revelacioun of *Joon* the Apocalips		with	xxii.

Thus all these Pistlis stonden in her ordre.

* MSS. *Caius & Emanuel A. D.* 1397.

Contents page of the Wyclifite
New Testament dated 1397.

THE

NEW TESTAMENT,

WITH

The Lessons

TAKEN OUT OF

THE OLD LAW,

READ IN CHURCHES ACCORDING TO THE USE OF SARUM;

TRANSLATED

INTO ENGLISH FROM THE VULGAR LATIN.

BY JOHN WICLIF, D. D.

RECTOR OF LUTTERWORTH, 1380.

social disturbance. It is clear that many viewed him as the most prominent leader of the Reform party. The main objects of his attack: Papal interference and church property. His chief enemies: the bishops.

Oxford supported John Wyclif until 1380 when his attacks on transubstantiation made him an embarrassment. Even John of Gaunt, who had his own reasons for wishing to humiliate the church, felt obliged to back off a little towards the end.

In his treatise *Objections to the Friars* Wyclif argued powerfully against the sale of indulgences, thus anticipating Luther by one-and-a-half centuries. 'There is no pardon but of God,' insisted Wyclif. No wealth on earth, he argued, could buy forgiveness of sins. 'May God destroy the pride, covetousness, hypocrisy and heresy of this feigned pardoning,' he fulminated, 'and make men busy to keep his commandments, and to set fully their trust in Jesus Christ.' Wyclif earned the title Victorian historians were to give him: 'The Morning Star of the Reformation'.

The very causes that attracted to him the hostility of church authorities, ensured him a following among the common people. Soon he was perceived as their champion. In the last five years of his life he attracted a considerable following of 'poor priests'. These 'Lollards' went about preaching to the common people.

Three papal bulls drafted on the same day were soon chasing him. One was sent to the Archbishop of Canterbury, another to the University of Oxford, and the third to the King. All indicted the Rector of Lutterworth, John Wyclif, for 'most wicked and damnable heresies'. In fact the bishops had instituted proceedings before the papal bulls had arrived. In February 1377 Wyclif was ordered to appear in Our Lady's Chapel in St. Paul's to face the consequences of his words and deeds.

Wyclif's reception by the populace in London must have

done much to lift his spirits. It was only with the greatest of difficulty that he, with his two patrons — John of Gaunt, Duke of Lancaster, and Lord Percy, Earl Marshal of England — could force their way through the massive throng surrounding St. Paul's.

It was made very clear to both Wyclif and his protectors that he was standing trial.

In no time the trial had to be abandoned.

The mob burst in, and uproar ensued.

Wyclif did not wait for another hearing but returned to Oxford.

Before many months passed the fact of his popular standing was to become apparent again. Parliament was debating the issue of the Papacy's distraint of revenue from England. Parliament called upon Wyclif to give his opinion on the matter and to argue it from the Scriptures. His reply was well received. Parliament ended the outflow of revenue.

But the bishops were still more determined to bring the reformer to book after their experience at St. Paul's. This time Wyclif was summoned to Lambeth Palace. He went alone; his excursions into 'heresy' were embarrassing even John of Gaunt. But they were not embarrassing the mob who, once again, were out in force in favour of their champion. The chapel where he was tried was chock full. Before proceedings were long under way an emissary arrived from Court. He carried a warrant for safe conduct signed by the Queen Mother. It forbade any sentence being passed on Wyclif.

The bishops knew when they were beaten.

The mob were jubilant as Wyclif walked triumphantly to freedom.

Back in Lutterworth he was committing to paper his defence. Of the divided Papacy he wrote: 'Now is the Head of Antichrist cloven in twain and one part contendeth against the other.' Echoes here of the preaching of a later era. In his pamphlet *On the Schism of the Popes* he openly stated his opposition to Papal authority. In his pamphlet *On the Truth and Meaning of Scripture* he argued the case for the supremacy of Scripture in matters of doctrine.

Wyclif the Translator

Doubt remains as to the exact date when Wyclif began his Bible translation. However, it is certain that by the time of the Papal Schism — 1378 — it was well under way.

At the height of the Reformation controversy of the sixteenth century, Sir Thomas More, in controversy with William Tyndale, would say that he had seen an English Bible that predated Wyclif's. The Catholic scholar *may* have been referring to a partial translation undertaken by Richard Rolle who died in 1349. More likely, however, was that More was unaware that *two* translations were associated with the name of John Wyclif. If this was the case, clearly he had seen the older one.

Wyclif began by translating the last book in Scripture: Revelation. This was followed by a 'Harmony of the Gospels': a single life of Christ made from an intelligent integration of material from all four gospel accounts.

His first New Testament was finished in 1380; in 1384 the whole Bible was completed. This is known as 'the earlier Wycliffite Bible'. Constantly in touch with both Oxford and London his work of translation from Latin to English was actually undertaken at Lutterworth. Without doubt he had the assistance of other scholars. Even the New Testament was not entirely his own work; and the greater part of the Old Testament was certainly translated by Nicholas Hereford, a colleague and friend from Oxford.

At this stage Wyclif seems to have been beyond the reach of the ecclesiastical authorities. Hereford was not. In 1382 he was summoned to London. He was excommunicated. To save his own life he fled to the Continent.

At the time of Hereford's flight the Old Testament was not quite complete. One of Wyclif's assistants brought it to completion. Hence the entire English Bible had been completed just prior to Wyclif's death at the end of 1384.

A study of this, the first 'Wycliffite' Bible, makes it obvious where Wyclif's translation left off and Hereford's translation began. Hereford used a pedantic, translator's English. Wyclif's style, by contrast, was free and colloquial. 'There can be no doubt', writes Sir Frederic Kenyon, 'that he had in his mind the common people, for whom his version was specially intended, and that he wrote in a style they could understand and appreciate.'[1]

The second 'Wycliffite' Bible made its appearance after his death. It represented a revision of the earlier translation. This later Bible was completed in 1388. It is generally assumed that John Purvey, one of Wyclif's closest friends, undertook the entire work of revision. About 170 copies of this version are still extant.

Neither 'Wycliffite' Bible was written with any ornamentation. The copies were essentially prepared for private use only. The Wycliffite Bibles were beamed at those who could not read Latin. There was never any thought that it would supplant the Vulgate for scholarly use. The original biblical languages, Greek and Hebrew, were not consulted.

Though every attempt was made by the bishops to impound and burn Wyclif's Bibles they continued to be copied throughout the fifteenth century. Wyclif's reforming views also survived him by many years. Indeed, following his death, the Poor Preachers (or Lollards) were even more active than beforehand. Wyclif's ideas sparked other reforming movements elsewhere; both Jerome of Prague and John Huss of Bohemia acknowledged their indebtedness to the English reformer.

Renaissance

In the mid-fifteenth century two events occurred, the effects of which would revolutionize the history of the Bible. First, in May 1453 the Turks stormed Constantinople. Second, in November 1454 the first dated product of the printing press emerged.

The fall of the Eastern Empire forced West many scholars learned in both Greek and Hebrew. Both languages were almost forgotten in Western Europe. As the Constantinople scholars settled in Italy and elsewhere they fuelled the Renaissance spirit of enquiry and an enthusiasm to read the classics — including the Bible — in their original languages. Soon in universities in Italy, Flanders and England, Greek and Hebrew were being revived. The way was opened up for the appearance of accurate vernacular Bibles based on the oldest available manuscripts in the original biblical languages.

Johann Gutenberg of Mainz (c. 1398-1468) is credited with the invention of printing. By August 1456 he had published his first Bible: Jerome's Latin Vulgate.

But the invention of printing not only made possible the propagation of the Scriptures, but helped to ensure their accuracy. The progressive corruption of texts through the inevitable errors of copyists was brought to an end. The realization of Wyclif's vision was within prospect: the Bible accessible to every man.

The earliest printed vernacular Bibles predated the Reformation. A German Bible was printed at Strassburg by Mentelin in 1466. Eighteen others were to be published before the first part of Luther's translation appeared in 1522. An Italian Bible was printed in Venice in 1471, a Dutch Bible in 1477, a French Bible at Lyons in 1478 and another about 1487. Caxton's *Golden Legend*, published in 1483, was the nearest England came to a printed vernacular Bible during the fifteenth century; it included a part of the Bible narrative in English. It did not, however, eclipse the work of John Wyclif.

The Eve of Reformation

John Wyclif and his followers had anticipated many of the key doctrines of the Protestant Reformation 150 years before it occurred. The 'obstinate North Country mind endowed with the subtleties of the Oxford schools'[3] had established a principle which became more and more widely accepted: an accessible Bible as the only way to, and foundation of, truth. Wyclif also placed squarely on the shoulders of the temporal rulers the responsibility for reforming the church. Within a few years of his death his doctrines developed 'a widespread appeal among townsmen, merchants, gentry and even among some of the lower clergy'.[4]

In the course of the fifteenth century persecution forced Lollardy underground. During his lifetime Wyclif had seemed near to court; unquestionably he had powerful protectors. Following his death these protectors distanced themselves from the movement to which he had given rise. Nevertheless, the 'inspiration' of English heresy 'was overwhelmingly Wyclif, at least until about 1530'.[5] A steady stream of Lollards and Lollard Bibles were being burned until the very eve of the English Reformation.[6]

References
[1] K. B. McFarlane, *Wyclif and English Nonconformity* (1972), pages 78, 79.
[2] Sir Frederic Kenyon, *Our Bible and the Ancient Manuscripts* (1939), page 204.
[3] A. G. Dickens, *The English Reformation* (1967), page 41.
[4] Ibid, page 42.
[5] Ibid, page 47.
[6] Ibid, pages 48-62.

12

Outlawed!

What made Bible translation at once imperative and controversial was the Reformation.

Reformers believed that the most effective way to destroy the authority of the Roman Church was to give the people a Bible they could read for themselves. In Germany — the birthplace of the Reformation movement — the popular version was made by Luther. Returning from Worms where he had appeared before the Emperor, Luther was the victim of a stage-managed kidnapping. Luther's prince, Frederick the Wise of Saxony, decided that his protégé should, for safety's sake, be kept out of sight for a time. Luther was taken to the castle at Wartburg. This enforced isolation gave him the space for his translation.

In England, Bible translation would be undertaken in the face of the opposition of both church *and* prince. It would ultimately be the work of many hands. But one above all: William Tyndale.

A Forbidden Book

More than a century earlier (in July 1408), and as a reaction to the popularity of the Wyclif Bible, a comprehensive prohibition by the authorities had ordained 'that no one henceforth on his own authority (shall) translate any text of Holy Scripture into English'. It also made illegal the use or distribution of the version 'recently composed in the time of John Wyclif'.[1]

But Wyclif had given the English a taste for Scripture that neither prohibition nor time diminished. Indeed, 130 years after Wyclif's death 'the equivalent of £40' was given for a single copy of his Bible. 'Some gave a load of hay for a few chapters of St. James or St. Paul in English.'[2]

Wyclif's Bible, with the passage of time, had acquired two handicaps. One, because it came via the Latin it was inaccurate. Two, because of its illegality it had never been printed. The Reformation movement made necessary a new English translation that would harness Renaissance knowledge and technology.

What gave William Tyndale the text from which to translate was a Greek New Testament published in 1516 by Renaissance scholar Erasmus.

But what gave him the vision?

The story of Tyndale has all the ingredients of a spy thriller. One man's passion for a forbidden Book. Agents and double agents. Kings, popes, monks and cardinals. Constant danger and pursuit. Hairbreadth escapes under cover of darkness. Villains and traitors. And a hero with endless courage.

Decision in the Great Hall

Tyndale came of farming stock and was born in Gloucestershire. Despite the role that life made him play he was by instinct a modest, quiet scholar. After spending five years at Oxford and three at Cambridge he left university and directed his footsteps to a village nestling on the slopes of the Cotswold hills, near his place of birth. He spent the next eighteen months in the employment of the squire of Little Sodbury, Sir John Walsh. He worked as tutor to the squire's children. It was in the great hall of the manor house at Little Sodbury that his destiny was decided.

Sir John was a local dignitary. The great hall of his manor house saw many a distinguished guest. In the long winter evenings all kinds of important men would sit at Sir John's long oak table, including the odd bishop. Between those walls, adorned with weapons of war, these men sat and discussed the great issues of the day. The revolutionary preaching of Luther of Wittenberg was the centre of the controversy.

As an educated man Tyndale took part in their discussions. Indeed, he was often at the heart of the debate. On religious issues he tended to disagree with the other guests. He knew the Bible so well that he often beat them down with argument.

On one memorable evening when the discussion was particularly heated one scholar, thus beaten down, shouted: 'We had better be without God's laws than the Pope's.' In reply, slowly and deliberately, Tyndale uttered the fateful words: 'I defy the Pope and all his laws. If God spare my life ere many years I will cause a boy that driveth the plough shall know more of the Scripture than thou doest.'

To London

A few days later Tyndale had his first brush with the authorities. He had been preaching at College Green, Bristol, and fallen foul of the local priests. [3] Before a local court he was charged with heresy. To fulfil his ambition of translating the New Testament into English and realizing that he could not remain a free man for long in that part of the country, Tyndale set out on his long trek to distant London.

London had printing presses. It also had the advantage, Tyndale believed, of an enlightened bishop. Cuthbert Tunstall was a scholar and a friend of Erasmus. 'Then thought I, if I might come to this man's service, I were happy,' wrote Tyndale later, 'and so I gat me to London.'

He arrived in the mid-summer of 1523. In his pocket he carried a letter of introduction from Sir John Walsh to the Controller of the Royal household. In his heart he carried the hope that somehow an interview with Bishop Tunstall could be arranged and his support secured for his plan to translate the New Testament, and in the end the whole Bible, into current English. The financial and moral backing of the Bishop of London could make or break his plans.

No room in all England!

Finally, after many weeks, when August had mellowed into September, he obtained an interview with the Bishop. The half-light of late evening found the translator trudging into the courtyard of the Bishop's palace and pulling the huge bell that hung at the side of the massive weather-beaten door. Soon he was seated in the audience chamber. The light of the setting sun streamed in through the latticed windows, making chequered the sombre garb of the Bishop of London. Soon the sun was to set for ever on Tyndale's fortunes in England.

The Bishop did not say much. His favour at court was good. The project was risky. From the moment he entered the Bishop's chamber Tyndale knew his hopes were dashed. In Germany Martin Luther, having produced a German Bible, was leading the attack against the Catholic Church. The Bishop was afraid that Tyndale aimed to do the same in England. And so, wrote Tyndale: 'My lord answered me that his house was full, and advised me to seek in London, where he said I could not lack service.' Tunstall was, Tyndale decided, 'a ducking hypocrite, made to dissemble'.

As the shadows of night deepened he trudged the darkened streets, his hopes and dreams blasted. The money given him by Sir John was spent. He was penniless. But Tyndale believed that God had given him a task to do. Hence he ventured to believe that God would give him the means to do it. This he found in the home of a rich cloth merchant of Barking, one Humphrey Monmouth, a travelled and generous-hearted man.

Monmouth took Tyndale in after he had heard him preach. Later he would testify: 'I took him into my house half a year; and there he lived like a good priest. . . . He studied most part of the day and of the night at his book.'

Tyndale was, in fact, working on the first draft of his New Testament. But he knew that if his work were ever to be published he must seek another land. In the house of Monmouth he met many wealthy merchants who were to provide vital assistance in future days. They were part of the international world of Lutheranism and 'were certainly linked with men of Lollard background'.[4] In one of their ships he was soon leaving the shores of England behind. If his work of translation were to be completed and published he must seek other, more congenial shores. In May 1524 he sailed for Hamburg, never to return.

'Not only was there no room in my Lord of London's palace to translate the Scriptures,' he said, 'but there was no room in all England.'

Under Cover

After the merchantman docked at Hamburg mystery covers Tyndale's movements. His story takes on even more the atmosphere of a modern spy thriller — secret comings and goings, under-cover meetings, narrow escapes, spies, agents and a traitor within the gates. . . . Tyndale and his accomplices were in constant fear of detection and of their lives. Strange; and all the stranger when one considers what they were trying to do — translate and publish an English Bible.

Sources hostile to Tyndale suggest that he matriculated at the University of Wittenberg on 27 May 1524. While the motive behind this allegation is to create an association between Tyndale and Luther, Wittenberg was the obvious place to go. Luther was back from Wartburg, his German Bible published. Wittenberg's Professor of Greek was Philip Melanchthon, and its Professor of Hebrew, Aurogallus. While Tyndale already had a scholar's knowledge of both languages and at least part of

an English New Testament in manuscript form, the advice
of such scholars and access to their libraries would have been
of tremendous help. Certainly Tyndale would have found at
Wittenberg an atmosphere suitable for the work of translation.

While at Wittenberg he employed runaway friar William
Roye as a secretary and 'manager'. On Tyndale's own description Roye was something of a rascal. But his assistance and
cunning were to prove an asset.

By the spring of 1525 the New Testament had been translated into English. The first part of the job was done. Now
for the second part: Where should it be printed and who
should print it? Anything coming from Wittenberg was suspect. Cologne, on the other hand, had many printers and was
in a far better position for shipping the printed works to
England. Around the hearth of Humphrey Monmouth in
Barking, Tyndale had hatched a plan with sympathetic merchants. His Bibles would be smuggled into England packed
in bales of cloth and other merchandise. Cologne was ideal
for putting this plan into action.

In August 1525 he arrived in Cologne still accompanied by
his useful, if not altogether honest friend Roye. In that city
of spires and turrets, sloping down to the Rhine, they had
little difficulty in contacting a printer. Peter Quentel was willing to undertake the venture in the strictest secrecy. Soon the
type was set up, and preparation was made to print 3,000
copies.

The Traitor

During this period of preparation Tyndale had been in a
constant state of tension. This was a vital stage. All that was
required was for one person to report to the authorities and
life and labours would be lost. News was coming through from
England of a new spate of burnings. The Emperor Charles
V was eager to stamp out heresy in Germany. His agents were

everywhere. It was a desperate gamble. Would it pay off? Hearts thumped hard as the first sheets were taken off the press. The first two gospels were almost completed when the word came: 'Stop work!'

The thundering voice came from an army officer whose form filled the printing house doorway. Beyond him could be seen the glint of steel.

The powers from which Tyndale had escaped in England had been anything but asleep. The informer had been John Cochlaeus, a fanatic who had pledged himself to destroy anything that sounded like Reformation and to use any means to do so. He had tailed Tyndale and Roye from Wittenberg to Cologne, and infiltrated his way into Quentel's printing house and into the confidence of the printers. At work they talked little of the project in hand, but in the beer halls of Cologne in the evenings he found that tongues were loosened. Whether King Henry and Cardinal Wolsey wanted it or no, England would soon have a Reformation! He listened more attentively. And when the evening wore on and secret whisperings became a raucous hubbub he learned more. Two Englishmen . . . skilful in languages . . . a Testament in English! He pressed still closer. These Englishmen, who were they? But then mouths closed like vices. The fracas subsided, stares were hostile. The informer disappeared into the night.

But Cochlaeus had not given up. Pretending to be supervising another print job he again gained access to Quentel's printing house. He became acquainted with some of the master craftsmen and invited them to his lodgings. Beer was tippled and tongues were loosened. In Cochlaeus's own words, 'One of them in private conversation disclosed to me the secret by which England was to be won over to the party of Luther.' Bibles were already being printed in English. Costs were being met by wealthy London merchants who were to smuggle them into England and disperse them throughout the country before King and Cardinal could discover or prohibit it. Cochlaeus, having no further use for his guests, left them in their stupor and immediately contacted a city senator — Herman Rinck. Rinck was well known to the Emperor and the King of England. Distrusting Cochlaeus, however, Rinck planted another spy in the printing house, and from him received confirmation of the tale. Hence it was that on the authority of the Senate of Cologne that the thundering voice of the Commander halted Quentel's printing works.

Flight

Tyndale and Roye immediately sensed danger. It was not only the printed sheets that the senator would wish to seize! Hurriedly, before the soldiers entered, Tyndale gathered the already printed ten sheets and the pair left by a back entrance, making for the river. A fragment of Tyndale's New Testament printed at Quentel's (Matthew chapters 1-22) was discovered in 1834 and is now in the British Museum.

For the second time Tyndale's hopes had been dashed and his plans blighted. The traitor within the gates had done his work. Now fresh plans must be made, and made quickly! If their lives and manuscripts were to be preserved they must fly!

Meanwhile Rinck and Cochlaeus were composing letters to Henry VIII and Cardinal Wolsey. The 'wicked enterprise' of Tyndale and his friends was disclosed, and warning was given that English sea ports must take precautions against the entrance of this 'pernicious merchandise'.

References
[1] Cited, H. W. Robinson (ed), *The Bible in its Ancient and English Versions* (1940), pages 148, 149.
[2] Ibid, pages 147, 148.
[3] A. G. Dickens, *The English Reformation* (1967), page 105.
[4] Ibid, page 106.

Martyred

Tyndale and Roye waited in the warehouses at the Cologne quayside for night to fall.

When the sunset had melted on the restless Rhine, Tyndale and Roye emerged from their lair and 'took ship' up river.[1]

Smuggled to England

They must have travelled by water for some days. They would have passed Bonn, Coblenz and Mainz as the Rhine corridored through the steep defile of vine-clad, castle-capped hills.

Tyndale put ashore at Worms, a Protestant city. It was October. Here he contacted a printer, Peter Schoeffer, and without loss of time his printing presses began rolling off English New Testaments.

On 11 August 1526 Spalatinus, secretary to the Elector of Saxony, dined with Buschius, a well-known Renaissance scholar. That night he made this entry in his diary: 'Buschius told us that 6,000 copies of the New Testament have been printed in English. The work has been translated by an Englishman staying there with two other Britons who is so skilful in seven languages — Hebrew, Greek, Latin, Italian, Spanish, English and French — that whichever he speaks you would think it his native tongue.'[2]

Tyndale had been in Germany two years. Now 6,000 copies of the New Testament in English had been run off the presses at Worms. It was time for Monmouth and his merchant friends to play their part in shipping the testaments into English ports concealed in their cargoes. Hidden beneath bales of cloth, flour and other commodities, English New Testaments were being smuggled into England by the thousand.

Two copies of the Worms octavo survive; one at the Baptist college in Bristol, the other in the library at St. Paul's.

Despite Cardinal Wolsey's best efforts a flourishing trade sprang up. In England 'distributing agencies' were already in place to be activated. The English Testaments from the Continent were soon finding eager buyers.[2]

Burning the Bible

Tunstall and his fellow bishops were enraged. A fresh hue and cry for Tyndale and Roye was raised on the Continent. Movements had to be concealed. In August 1526 in England, a conclave of bishops resolved to 'burn all untrue translations of the Scriptures', and appointed Tunstall to strike at the centre of distribution — London.

Soon Tunstall, to the roar of the flames as they consumed the first English Testaments, was thundering out his famous sermons from St Paul's Cross. Few listened. But the flames continued avidly to devour.

While Tunstall was busy Bible-burning at St. Paul's Cross, Archbishop Warham was buying up as many copies as he could lay his hands on. In one instance £70 was spent on one batch alone. This keen 'demand' from the Bible's enemies and their readiness to pay a good price stimulated the printers to fresh efforts, and soon Bibles were flooding the English coast in even greater quantities. The fact that, by now, Tyndale's translation had been pirated several times in Holland only served to increase the inundation. Tyndale, however, complained that the pirated versions might at least have made more strenuous efforts after accuracy.

In 1529 England signed a treaty in Antwerp. Tunstall was sent to represent the government. Knowing Antwerp to be an important centre of dispatch for Tyndale Testaments he made under-cover enquiries among the merchants as to the sources of supply. In doing so he came across a London merchant called Augustin Packington. Packington seemed willing to do business, and Tunstall revealed his plan to buy up the Testaments. Packington was, it seemed, in an excellent position to buy up Tyndale Testaments and professed himself willing and able to fall in with the bishop's plans 'provided he had the wherewithal'. The bishop was jubilant. At last the heretical testament would be removed from circulation. He would have been less jubilant had he known that Packington, a good friend of Tyndale's, was actually the kingpin in the plan by which Testaments were being smuggled into England.

He lost no time in acquainting Tyndale with his 'deal with the bishop'. 'I have gotten thee a merchant,' he said, 'which with ready money shall dispatch thee of all that thou hast!'

'Who is the merchant?' enquired Tyndale.

'The Bishop of London!'

The Bishop of London!

Now Tyndale was jubilant. His debts could be paid, and a revised edition of the New Testament launched. The bargain was struck.

When Tunstall, at a later date, complained to the sharp-witted Packington that the flow of Bibles into England had not ceased, Packington professed that he had done his part, but if the Bishop would stem the flow he must buy up the printing presses. Tunstall realized that he had had the worst end of the bargain.

The truth was eventually ferreted out by England's new Chancellor, Sir Thomas More, from a man called George Constantine.

'My Lord,' said Constantine, 'will you that I tell you the truth? It is the Bishop of London that hath helpen us; for he bestoweth among us a great deal of money . . . and that is our only succour and comfort.'

On the Run

While Tyndale's venture prospered, his enemies defied and outwitted, the campaign for his capture was speeded up.

Between 1527 and 1530 almost total mystery surrounds his whereabouts. By May 1527 Wolsey's agent in Antwerp, Hackett, was reporting that someone was translating the Old Testament into English. After the publication of the New Testament it is, in fact, likely that Tyndale remained for some time in Worms where he could have ready access to the Hebrew manuscripts. During this period he parted finally — and willingly — from his companion Roye. A renewed outbreak of persecution in England made it necessary to 'lie low'.

It was dangerous to be a Protestant, let alone a Protestant with known reformist views — *and* a Bible translator. In England Sir Thomas More had lighted the fires of Smithfield and many a Protestant martyr had been burned. Tyndale's life was lived in constant awareness that any day, any moment, his whereabouts and identity would be discovered by an English or an Imperial agent, and that he would add more human fuel to the flames.

Shipwrecked

During this period, too, he suffered another major setback. In Marburg he had continued in his work of translating the first five books of the Old Testament. When it became apparent that enemy agents had tailed him to Marburg he set out on a midnight flight to Antwerp. Alone, and carrying only his books and copies, he set out on foot. He could travel only by night and even then he avoided the main highways and skirted towns where possible.

He had not been in Antwerp long before it too became unsafe for him. This time he boarded a ship for Hamburg where he hoped to have his translation of the Pentateuch published.

But, in the words of Bishop Foxe, 'Off the coast of Holland the ship was wrecked and he lost all his books, writings and copies, and so was compelled to begin anew.'

More than a year's work destroyed! He was saved. How, we do not know. But we *do* know that on his return to Antwerp he sailed again for Hamburg right away. He had faced difficulties before. This was no time for despair.

In Hamburg he met Miles Coverdale, recently arrived from Cambridge, who eventually was to complete his work for him. With Coverdale's assistance he began the process of retranslating the first five books of the Bible. The work was finally completed and published by John Hoochstraten in Antwerp, 17 January 1530.

In the months ahead he tackled a translation of the book of Jonah, very popular at that time. He also translated, but did not publish, the historical books of the Old Testament (Joshua to 2 Chronicles). In the course of the year following his publication of the Pentateuch he returned to Antwerp.

Safe passage to England?

Meanwhile changes were afoot in England. To achieve his divorce from Catherine of Aragon so that he could marry Anne Boleyn, Henry VIII had separated the English Church from the Church of Rome. In doing so he had made *himself* the head of the English Church. This turn-round in affairs in England also resulted in a turn-round in England's attitude towards Tyndale. Could his powerful pen be enlisted in the Royal cause? Despite Tyndale's condemnation of the divorce, King Henry was persuaded by Thomas Cromwell to offer him safe conduct to England.[4]

The tricky assignment of making contact with Tyndale was given to a merchant called Stephen Vaughan. Repeated attempts were made to contact Tyndale, but without success. Where he was remained unknown.

Tyndale's friends told him about Vaughan's mission. After a while Vaughan was approached in the street and informed that a man was willing to meet him. To the messenger Vaughan replied, 'Who is your friend and where is he?'

'His name I know not, but if it be your pleasure to go where he is I will be glad thither to bring you,' replied the messenger.

Still no wiser, Vaughan was led through one of the worst parts of Antwerp — until they reached the edge of the city. Outside the city gates he left Vaughan. Looking around him, Vaughan could see no one until, when all was silence, a skinny form emerged from the shadows of the city wall.

'My name is Tyndale. . . .'

But he shook his head at the offer of safe passage. His work was not yet completed. Safe passage to England? The currents were still too changeable. The lean figure of Tyndale receded into the shadows. Vaughan was left with only a message for King Henry, and in that message the dearest hope of the man who had written it:

'If it would stand with the King's most gracious pleasure to grant only a bare text of the Scripture to be put forth among his people . . . be it of the translation of what person soever shall please His Majesty, I shall immediately make faithful promise never to write more, nor abide two days in these parts after the same; but immediately to repair unto his realm and humbly submit myself at the feet of His Royal Majesty, offering my body to suffer what pain or torture, yea, what death His Grace will, so that this be obtained.'

Vaughan passed from the scene. Persuasion was again replaced by force, and the English ambassador to the Netherlands was issued with a directive to the effect, 'Get Tyndale, dead or alive!'

The Closing of the Net

But Tyndale had vanished. Somewhere he was engaged in revising his translation of the New Testament, but where no one knew. His revised editions were published in 1534 and 1535. The fires of Smithfield burned fiercely. In their fury Tyndale now lost some of his best friends.

As 1534 faded Tyndale was living at the house of an English merchant in Antwerp whose name was Thomas Poyntz. He was bringing his final revision of the New Testament to a close. Outside the storm clouds were gathering. The Emperor Charles V was determined to wipe out heresy in the Netherlands.

The end for Tyndale was to come about by a train of events initiated by Tunstall's successor as Bishop of London. His death was at the hands of the Imperial authorities.

The first dark shadows fell across Tyndale's path in the summer of 1535. The shadow was that of a man — Henry Phillips. A gambler, he had fallen on difficult times in London. In order to win back his fortune he had become a secret agent. His mission was to bring about the arrest of Tyndale.

Tyndale was completely fooled when Phillips first presented himself at the house of Thomas Poyntz. He invited him into the house and even secured him a night's lodging showing him his translation. But Poyntz was not so easily fooled. Phillips soon learned that he would get no help from him.

His chance came when Poyntz went away on a six-week business trip. Phillips invited Tyndale to dine. Tyndale accepted. When he went to collect his guest Phillips had the house surrounded with guards, with two on either side of the door to collar the unsuspecting Tyndale as soon as he emerged.

The corridor that led to the door of Poyntz's house at Antwerp was so narrow that the two men could not walk abreast, and Phillips pushed Tyndale on ahead. Being taller than Tyndale, Phillips, as one source has it, 'pointed with his finger over Tyndale's head down at him, that the officers on either side of the door might get the right man'. A few paces from the door, Tyndale saw the Spanish soldiers and stopped. But it was too late. The little man was carried bodily out of the door by Phillips.

Vilvorde

Later that day the drawbridge of the castle of Vilvorde closed behind him. The huge walls of Vilvorde made freedom seem a thousand miles away. Outside, the feeble hands of Poyntz defied them. Frantic attempts were made on Tyndale's behalf. But the evil genius of Henry Phillips again took a hand in the proceedings and Poyntz narrowly escaped arrest.

Tyndale's arrest had taken place in May 1535. The ensuing eighteen months were employed in writing his defence. But, in fact, the drawbridge had closed for ever. By October 1535 there was a chill in the air. The cells at Vilvorde became even more dark and dismal.

Towards the end of the year Tyndale wrote a letter to the authorities requesting 'a warmer cap'. He wrote, 'I suffer extremely from cold in the head, being afflicted with perpetual catarrh.' He asked too for a warmer coat, a patch for his leggings and, most of all, a Hebrew Bible and Hebrew grammar to pursue his translation. Whether he got them we do not know.

His requests were similar to those made in the letter that Paul smuggled to Timothy from his Roman prison. He, too, wanted his 'scrolls and parchments' — and a heavy overcoat to withstand the winter. Like Tyndale, Paul had looked back on a life of escapes, arrests and shipwreck.

When Tyndale next emerged into the light of day it was on 6 October 1536. He was led to the centre of an enclosure at Vilvorde. Projecting through a small platform was a massive wooden cross. Round his throat was a loose-fitting rope, and around his neck and feet an iron chain secured him to the stake. On a signal from an officer the rope was tightened. When the flames began to lick his clothing Tyndale was already dead. On his lips was the immortal cry: *'Lord, open the King of England's eyes!'*

If Tyndale's death cry reflected his request to Henry VIII through Vaughan it was answered before it was uttered. Before the end of 1535, the previous year, in England the Bible Tyndale loved made its first semi-official appearance. Soon it bore the signature 'Henry Tudor'. The style of this Bible, as of many that came after it, was the style of Tyndale. Tyndale's memorial: The Bible in English.

The last letter in Tyndale's handwriting, as he lay in the dark cell at Vilvorde, concluded with the words: 'I shall be patient, abiding the will of God, to the glory and the grace of my Lord and Saviour, Jesus Christ.' A reflection, surely, of the letter of that other condemned prisoner, the apostle Paul, whose life so closely resembles Tyndale's: *'For I am now ready to be offered, and the time of my departure is at hand. I have fought a good fight, I have finished my course, I have kept the faith: henceforth there is laid up for me a crown of glory.'*

References
[1] F. F. Bruce, *The English Bible* (1961), page 31.
[2] Cited, J. Isaacs, 'The Sixteenth Century English Versions', H. W. Robinson (ed), *The Bible in its Ancient and English Versions* (1940), page 153.
[3] Ibid.
[4] A. G. Dickens, *The English Reformation* (1967), page 111.

Towards King James

Before Tyndale was strangled and burned, his erstwhile enemy Sir Thomas More was beheaded. His sensitive conscience had not permitted him to follow his King through the policy of divorcing his Queen and separating from Rome. More and Tyndale, giants of their age, had spent years in argument, attacking and counter-attacking in pamphlet warfare. Now both were dead.

More's replacement as Chancellor of England was Thomas Cromwell. Architect of the Tudor state, the subtle, political mind of Cromwell was also bent towards Reformation. The English Bible had made its semi-authorized appearance, having been brought together by Tyndale's disciple Miles Coverdale. Coverdale was under the direct patronage of Thomas Cromwell.

Coverdale's Bible

In December 1534 Thomas Cranmer, Archbishop of Canterbury, through the Convocation of Canterbury, petitioned the King to decree 'that the Holy Scripture shall be translated into the vulgar English tongue by certain upright and learned men to be named by the said most illustrious King'.

Coverdale's Bible made its appearance just twelve months after Cranmer's petition. It was the first complete English Bible and, while not strictly 'authorized', it was dedicated to Henry VIII. It was printed in Zurich.

Coverdale had produced his Bible in something of a hurry. Miles Coverdale (1488-1568) was an altogether more amenable character than Tyndale. In his preface he freely admitted his indebtedness to other translators (but not until the 1550 edition did he screw up the courage actually to name William Tyndale as one of them). But no one was under any illusions. Tyndale's style was too distinctive. Coverdale used all of Tyndale's work he could lay his hands on and, for the rest, he completed the translation himself from German and Latin Bibles.

When the second edition of Coverdale's Bible appeared in 1537 it was printed in England and actually licensed by the King. Over the next seventy-five years the work of revising and improving the Bible was almost continuous. 'Throughout, the work of Tyndale formed the foundation, and more than anyone else he established the rhythms and furnished much of the language which is familiar to us in our Authorized Version.'[1]

'Matthew's Bible'

As with the first edition of Coverdale's Bible in 1535, 'Matthew's Bible' of 1537 made its appearance as a result of the combined pressure of Thomas Cromwell and Thomas Cranmer. It received a royal licence.

Its popular name derived from the fact that the name Thomas Matthew appeared in its preface. It is likely that there was no such person and that John Rogers, who edited 'Matthew's Bible', used a false name to cover his tracks in case the King should once again change his mind about vernacular Bibles.[2] The alternative theory is that 'Thomas Matthew' was simply a pseudonym for Tyndale whose name was still anathema at court.[3] Certainly Matthew's Bible was the one most closely associated with Tyndale. It silently incorporated Tyndale's unpublished version of the historical books of the Old Testament. Less wisely it incorporated too many of Tyndale's provocative prefaces and annotations.

In fact Rogers had brought together a composite. The Pentateuch, the historical books from Joshua to 2 Chronicles and the whole of the New Testament were Tyndale's; most of the remainder was Coverdale's work.

Neither of the two rival authorized editions of 1537 was entirely satisfactory. Coverdale's Bible made good reading but the sections he had translated himself were notoriously distant from the original texts. 'Matthew's Bible', containing as it did Tyndale's provocative annotations, was too controversial.

The Great Bible

Towards the end of 1537 Thomas Cromwell gave Coverdale the task of 'cleaning up' and revising 'Matthew's Bible'. Thus work began on the Great Bible which was to make its appearance in 1539 and supersede the earlier 'authorized' Bibles.

To prepare the way for its arrival the clergy were charged on 5 September 1538: 'That ye shall provide, on this side of the Feast of All Saints next coming, one book of the whole Bible of the largest volume in English, and the same set up in some convenient place within the said church that ye have cure of, whereas your parishioners may most commodiously resort to the same and read it.'

Hence when the Great Bible appeared in 1539 it became the first formally authorized Bible for public use. Thomas Cranmer wrote its preface. But it was essentially Coverdale's revision of Matthew's Bible which was, in turn, John Roger's revision of Tyndale's Bible.

It was an instant success. Vast crowds gathered around the six copies which were set up in St. Paul's Cathedral. It ran through seven editions in two years.[4]

In the final years of his reign — 1540-1547 — Henry VIII reacted against moves towards Reformation. Thomas Cromwell was executed. But there was no dampening the English enthusiasm for the Bible. Some parishioners found the Great Bible so fascinating that they were reading aloud from it during divine service. The King had to issue a proclamation against this practice so that the priest could make himself heard!

Under Edward VI editions of Tyndale's, Coverdale's and the Great Bible poured from the presses. Mary's accession in 1553 put an end to this. Thomas Cranmer, Hugh Latimer and John Rogers paid the ultimate price for their enthusiasm for Protestantism and the English Bible.

The Geneva Bible

Many English-Bible enthusiasts sought exile in Geneva during Mary's reign. Here work on Bible translation continued. The Geneva translators were happy with Tyndale's New Testament and the portion of the Old Testament translated by Tyndale. Hence their work was concentrated on that section of the Old Testament that Tyndale's arrest and imprisonment had prevented him from tackling. The Geneva New Testament was published in 1557 and the complete Geneva Bible in 1560. The greatest contribution of the Geneva Bible is an Old Testament entirely translated from Hebrew.

From a modern standpoint the most unfortunate thing about the Geneva Bible is the quantity of sectarian notes. These were unashamedly Calvinistic in doctrine and served as an irritant to, among others, the future James I. Nevertheless, for half a century, the peoples of both England and Scotland read the Geneva Bible in preference to any other version and learned their theology from the appended notes.

Another novelty about the Geneva Bible was that it was divided into verses. The Hebrew Old Testament had first been divided into verses by Rabbi Nathan in 1448. The first Bible to contain the present verse divisions in both testaments had been Stephanus's Vulgate of 1555. The Geneva Bible simply followed these verse divisions.

The Geneva Bible became the household Bible of English-speaking Protestants in both England and Scotland. Since John

Knox had been one of the Geneva exiles before leading the Scottish Reformation it was natural that the Geneva Bible should be the version appointed to be read in Scottish churches.

Even when other Bibles had come along, including the King James version of 1611, the Geneva Bible held on to its devotees in both England and Scotland. When Oliver Cromwell's New Model Army went into battle in the English civil wars of the 1640s they took with them a copy of the Soldiers' Pocket Bible (the Geneva Bible under a new title).

The Geneva Bible was, by some, dismissed as the 'Breeches Bible'. The Geneva translators followed the Wycliffite versions in making Genesis 3:7 read that Adam and Eve sewed fig leaves together and made themselves 'breeches'.

The Bishops' Bible

At the time of Thomas Cromwell's execution in 1540 a project had been afoot to prepare a vernacular Bible under the direct supervision of the English bishops. It had come to nothing. In 1561 Elizabeth I's Archbishop of Canterbury, Matthew Parker, revived the idea. He submitted to the bishops a proposal that they should revise the Great Bible.

A scholar of considerable standing, Parker was eminently qualified to act as editor-in-chief. The actual work of translation, however, was 'subcontracted out' to a number of scholars, some of whom were already bishops and some of whom were to become bishops.

The 'Bishops' Bible' was completed in seven years and copies were sent to the Queen on 22 September 1568. The Convocation of Canterbury ordered that it should be used in all cathedrals and churches as far as possible.

King James

James I who acceded in 1603 had some pretensions to be a Bible scholar. As King James VI of Scotland he had already written a *Paraphrase upon the Revelation of St. John* and had translated the Psalms into metre.[5]

But James was prejudiced against the Geneva version. Since it was the first Bible ever published in Scotland (1579), given that it had been dedicated to him and having regard to the fact that it was the version from which he quoted in his own writings, his prejudice seems rather surprising. Almost certainly it was purely on the grounds that its margins were loaded with sectarian commentary.[6]

In January 1604, not long after the King's accession, the Hampton Court Conference was convened. Dr. John Reynolds, president of Corpus Christi College, Oxford, the leader of the Puritan wing of the Church of England, proposed that there be a new translation of the Bible.

The resolution passed was 'that a translation be made of the whole Bible, as consonant as can be to the original Hebrew and Greek; and this to be set out and printed, without any marginal notes, and only to be used in all churches of England in time of divine service'.

The King was enthusiastic. However, the clause regarding marginal notes was doubtless included on his insistence. 'I wish some special pains were taken for an uniform translation,' he said, 'which should be done by the best-learned men in both universities, then reviewed by the bishops, presented to the Privy Council, lastly ratified by royal authority to be read in the whole church and none other.'

The King himself took a leading part in organizing the work of translation. He undertook no translation himself. Six panels of translators (forty-seven men in all) had the work divided between them. Three panels were responsible for the Old Testament, two for the New, and one for the Apocrypha. Two of the panels met at Oxford, two at Cambridge and two at Westminster. When the panels had completed their work the draft translation was reviewed by a smaller group of twelve men, two from each panel, before the work was sent to the printer.

The payments made to the translators were tiny, but James promised them ecclesiastical preferment, and was as good as his word.

The King had drawn up the ground rules for the translators himself. The Bishops' Bible was to serve as the basis for the new translation. Marginal notes were to be used only to explain Hebrew and Greek words, to draw attention to parallel passages and to make the sense plainer. Words necessary to complete the sense of the text were to be printed in italics. Existing chapter and verse divisions were to be retained.

The Authorized Version made its appearance in 1611 and went through three editions within the year. There is a sense in which it represented Tyndale's dream fulfilled. Professor J. Isaacs has said: 'Tyndale's honesty, sincerity and scrupulous integrity, his simple directness, his magical simplicity of phrase, his modest music, has given an authority to his wording that has imposed itself on all later versions. With all the tinkering to which the New Testament has been subject, Tyndale's version is still the basis in phrasing, rendering, vocabulary and rhythm, and often in music as well. Nine tenths of the Authorized New Testament is still Tyndale, and the best is still his.'[7]

References
[1] Sir Frederic Kenyon, *The Story of the Bible* (1936), page 49.
[2] B. F. Westcott, *A General View of the History of the English Bible* (third edition 1905), pages 67, 68.
[3] J. Isaacs, 'The Sixteenth Century English Versions', H. W. Robinson (ed), *The Bible in its Ancient and English Versions* (1940), page 173.
[4] A. G. Dickens, *The English Reformation* (1967), page 190.
[5] J. Isaacs, 'The Authorised Version and After', H. W. Robinson (ed), *op cit*, page 197.
[6] F. F. Bruce, *The English Bible* (1961), page 97.
[7] J. Isaacs, *op cit*, pages 160, 204, 205.

After King James

The King James Bible

The King James Bible was attacked from all quarters as soon as it appeared.

Some preferred the Bishop's Bible. Many more preferred the Geneva Bible. There was a mood of intolerance.

The translators were not taken by surprise.

Up front the early editions of the King James Bible had a preface entitled 'The Translators to the Reader'. This preface was a humble appeal on the part of the translators to give the new version a fair chance. Their work had, said the translators, been 'welcomed with suspicion instead of love'. Interestingly for the time in which they wrote, the King James Bible translators exuded a very different spirit.

The translators of 'the King James' were very generous in their praise of previous translations: 'We are so far off from condemning the labours of those who travailed before us in this kind, either in this land or beyond sea, either in King Henry's time, or King Edward's . . . or Queen Elizabeth's of ever renowned memory; but we acknowledge them to have been raised up of God for the building and furnishing of his Church.'

Interesting.

In the last thirty years the tables have been turned. The supporters of the King James Bible have been attacking more modern versions. It is always a paradox to hear someone who loves and defends the King James version, opposing other translations. They are acting against the spirit of those who produced the Bible they are defending.

Of course, the King James Bible translators were on solid ground. They had merely 'obeyed the King's commandment. And what can the King command to be done that will bring him more true honour than this?' They had, they conceded, introduced many changes; but they expressed surprise that revision and correction should be 'imputed as faults'.

Of course, the King James version incorporated the chapter and verse divisions of earlier versions. It was also heavily punctuated. The chapter and verse divisions were meant to make Bible study easier. The punctuation was intended to make the sense easier to understand, and to enable those who read the Word in public to place the emphasis in the right places. It must be stated, however, that the 'beautiful' English of the KJV was never spoken English — at any time. To that extent it was always somewhat 'artificial'.

Inevitably early editions contained the odd misprint. None was more scandalous than the omission of the word 'not' from the seventh commandment in the 1631 edition. For this proof reader's error the King's printers were fined £300 by Archbishop Laud.

Catholic Versions

Before the publication of the King James Bible an English Bible had been produced for Roman Catholic readers. It had the approval of ecclesiastical authority and is generally referred to as the 'Douai Bible', after the place where it was translated.

Other Catholic Bibles have been produced in the twentieth century. Among the earliest of these was the translation of Ronald Knox.

The Latin Vulgate of Jerome was the basis for both the Douai and the Knox versions, rather than the Hebrew and

Greek texts (although Knox would appear to have kept the Hebrew and Greek in view throughout). The Douai translators were, to a large extent, cramped by a stand taken at the Council of Trent in 1546. It had laid down that this 'ancient and Vulgate version, which is approved by the long use of so many centuries in the Church herself, be held as authentic in public lectures, disputations, sermons and expository discourses, and that no one may make bold or presume to reject it on any pretext.'

Thus the Douai and Knox versions, based as they are on the Latin, may be held to follow the Wycliffite tradition of the English Bible. The Protestant versions, on the other hand, may be held to follow the Tyndale tradition.

Much of the credit for the Douai version must go to William Allan. Allan had been a fellow of an Oxford college who had refused to acquiesce in the Elizabethan religious settlement. Having fled to France he became the founder of an English college at Douai in 1568. The fact that the college was moved to Rheims in 1578 accounts for the fact that his version of the Bible is often termed the Douai-Rheims version.

The Douai-Rheims Bible was not nearly as inaccurate as most Protestants believed, and have continued to believe. In the manner of Tyndale there was a very full apparatus of annotations. But the great majority of these were of a non-theological character. They were intended to clear up difficulties and to interpret the text in conformity with the understanding of the translators. Only occasionally are they controversial and antagonistic.

By the mid-eighteenth century the Douai-Rheims version was largely unintelligible to most English-speaking Catholics. Therefore in 1749 Bishop Richard Challoner undertook a major revision. This in turn incorporated a work of revision undertaken in the previous century by Gregory Martin, also a member of the English college at Rheims.

King James: the need for revision

At the beginning of the twentieth century the King James Version, its Elizabethan English notwithstanding, was the one most commonly used in the English-speaking world. Nevertheless, as with the Catholic version, from the mid-eighteenth century demands for revision began to be heard. That these demands were muted and unrepresentative of the vast majority of Protestant Christians until well into the twentieth century, says much for the work done by the forty-seven men who worked under the direction of James I.

Indeed, at the time when the first demands for revision began to be heard, the King James version received its finest celebration in Handel's *Messiah*.

From the first the demands for revision were twofold: 1. The desire for a Bible in the 'English of the common man' to whom the lofty prose of the King James was unintelligible by the time the furnaces of the Industrial Revolution began to light the night sky. 2. The desire for greater textual accuracy.

In 1768 John Wesley issued a revised edition of the King James Bible with notes 'for plain, unlettered men who understand only their mother tongue'. Wesley based his revision on a careful study of the Greek original and made 12,000 revisions altogether. None of them, he assured his readers, was for alteration's sake.

However, what really fuelled demands for a revision of the King James Version was the discovery of no less than 4,500 manuscripts of the Greek New Testament — in whole or in part — most of which dated from a period much nearer to the apostles than the manuscripts from which Tyndale and subsequent translators had worked. Most notable of all, of course, was the discovery of the *Codex Sinaiticus*. 'It became increasingly clear that the Authorized Version required to be revised in order to be brought in closer conformity with the

Greek text of the New Testament, as established by more intensive textual study on the basis of more reliable evidence than
had been accessible in 1611.'[1]

Dr. A. Graham Maxwell, who has spent a life-time studying
the Greek Bible, has estimated that no less than 150,000
variants were discovered by scholars between the different
Greek manuscripts available. He is emphatic that none of them
alter either the picture of God which emerges from Scripture
or any fundamental Christiàn doctrine. Nevertheless it will
be understood that before this was clearly grasped — in the
last two decades of the nineteenth century — there was an
expressed desire on the part of many scholars to find out how
a translation of the earliest manuscripts would change their
understanding of Scripture.

As the man-in-the-pew became aware that the scholars were
undertaking detailed study of the most ancient Greek manuscripts with a view to a possible revised English Bible, he
began to worry.

In fact conscientious scholars, each one keeping a close eye
on the others' work, were burning midnight oil in Europe
and the United States of America. The newly-discovered
ancient manuscripts were each pored over as they were discovered. Whole life-times were spent in the pursuit of textual
accuracy. They were not in any way surprised to find variations
between the manuscripts. They could well imagine the difficulties involved in copying out the original Hebrew, Aramaic
and Greek. When the copyists were doing their work in the
early Christian centuries chapters and verses had not yet been
invented; there were no separations between the words (and,
therefore, there was the possibility of a number of different
ways of reading a particular collection of words); there was
no punctuation; in Hebrew there were no vowels!

What the scholars *were* surprised to discover was the minimal importance of the variations as they came to light. The

fact is that, while the wording frequently had to be altered, the understanding was hardly ever changed.[2]

What the discovery of the variations *did* provide, however, was an unassailable case for a revision of the King James Bible. Henry Alford, dean of Canterbury, began to argue in this way as early as 1869. A Royal Commission was established to revise the Authorized Version. In 1870, by the action of the Convocation of Canterbury, work was begun which would eventually lead to the publication of the Revised Version of 1881 and 1885. Members of the Church of Scotland and the English and Scottish free churches were represented on the translation committees. As the revision proceeded, American scholars were also involved.

It was, however, the British revisers who published the New Testament part of their work in May 1881, and the Old Testament part in May 1885. The upshot of the work of the American committee was not seen until 1901 when the American Standard Version was published.

Catholic revisions

Ronald Knox was not the only Roman Catholic involved in the production of a modern Bible.

Roman Catholic translators had a larger task than that of most Protestants. Though Jerome had had his doubts about the fourteen books of the Apocrypha back in AD 400, he had been told to include them in his Vulgate. Following his lead, some Protestant Bibles contained them beyond the Reformation. One of them was the King James Bible itself. After Luther, however, Protestant Bibles including the apocryphal books, placed them together between the two testaments. Roman Catholic Bibles, on the other hand, dispersed them through the Old Testament. There were even some Roman Catholic translators who looked longingly at the books of the Pseudepigrapha (the 'hidden books' with false titles) and even the very obviously fantastical apocryphal books of the New Testament. Nevertheless, the twenty-eight Roman Catholic scholars who produced *The Jerusalem Bible* in 1966 contented themselves with dispersing the fourteen books of the Apocrypha through the Old Testament in the traditional manner of Roman Catholic Bibles. Unlike previous Roman Catholic translations, however, *The Jerusalem Bible* was a translation from the original languages of the Bible, not from Jerome's Vulgate. The quality of their work brought many accolades from Protestant and Jewish scholars.

The New American Bible, also a Catholic translation, received accolades from non-Catholics.

Versions in modern English

The pedantic accuracy and precision with which those who produced the Revised Version of 1885 did their work made it an admirable version for the student. The variations found in the *Codex Sinaiticus* and the *Codex Vaticanus* were incorporated either in the text of the Revised Version or in the footnotes.

But there was still a problem: the old-fashioned language.

A. M. Hunter, writing in 1951, expressed the feeling of many scholars since the beginning of the century:

'Since the famous forty-seven did their work in 1611, nearly three-and-a-half centuries have passed. In that time our speech has so changed that the Authorised Version, for all the glories of its language, has grown more and more of a foreign tongue. The common man does not speak or properly understand the great accents of his Elizabethan ancestors. Were the Christian teacher or preacher concerned only with literary appreciation he might rest content with the Authorised Version, but his task, being what it is — to preach and teach the word of God to a generation that is almost biblically illiterate and slowly lapsing into paganism — he demands, and rightly demands, a version of the New Testament that will clothe the word of the Gospel in the vesture of our common speech, and come home with living power to men who do not understand, much less appreciate, the archaic splendours of Elizabethan prose.'[3]

Many scholars express the argument this way. The Greek in which the New Testament was written was not Classical Greek. It was the *koine*, the everyday language of the people. If the people of Paul's day could read the Scriptures in their everyday language, why should not the English-speaking people have the same privilege?

With modern speech and textual accuracy in mind, Dr. Richard Weymouth, a fellow of University College, London, having published a Greek New Testament, published *The New Testament in Modern Speech* in 1903. Sadly Weymouth's New Testament did not live up to the title he gave it. It contained a great deal of 'translators' English'; awkward, 'wooden' self-expression, together with many words and phrases long since dropped from ordinary speech. Nevertheless, Weymouth went through five editions. One of the plusses of his translation arose from his grasp of Paul's letters. By cutting down the long sentences of earlier versions he made the theology of the apostle Paul much easier to understand.

Arguably the breakthrough was made by the brilliant Scottish scholar Dr. James Moffatt. Moffatt published his New Testament in 1913, his Old Testament in 1924 and his complete one-volume Bible, *A New Translation of the Bible*, in 1928.

Moffatt's version was the one that really shocked the religious establishment. Though an academic, he had considerable grasp of secular language and was not afraid to use it in place of the pious language readers expected to find in their Bibles.

But Moffatt was first a scholar. Unlike Weymouth, his scholarship stretched to Hebrew as well as to Greek. Both languages came across in free and vigorous English. He gave English speakers their first taste of a really modern Bible.

In 1927 Moffatt's American counterpart, Dr. Edgar Goodspeed produced *The Complete Bible: An American Translation*. His rationalization for 'an American translation' was that even contemporary English 'familiar in England or Scotland' was 'strange in American ears'. In so far as this was an apology, it was unnecessary. Goodspeed contained less American idiom than Moffatt had Scottish idiom.

Recent translations

Before the outbreak of World War II the idea was floated that committees of British, American and Canadian scholars should work together on a new revision — in the light of recent manuscript discoveries and of changes in the use of English — of the Revised Version of 1885 and the *American Standard Version* of 1901. The war intervened, and the American and Canadian committees went to work on their own. The resultant *Revised Standard Version* was published in 1952. As with Goodspeed, the *Revised Standard Version* received as warm a welcome in Britain as it did in Canada and the United States. Unlike any previous version which traced its lineage back to King James, the *Revised Standard Version* finally abandoned *th* in favour of *s* in the ending of the third person singular of the present tense of verbs. Similarly thee and thou disappeared.

When the war ended there was, however, a different mood abroad in Britain. This mood affected the leadership of the Church of England, the Church of Scotland and the major Nonconformist denominations. The mood was against another mere revision of the Authorised Version and in favour of a completely new translation in modern speech.

It is likely that this mood had been sparked off in the war years by Dr. J. B. Phillips. Pastor of a parish which frequently experienced heavy night-time bombardment from the Luftwaffe, Phillips found that Christianity acquired a new relevance among his parishioners. His ideal was to infuse the youth of his congregation with this same sense of relevance. He set about doing this by introducing them to the letters of Paul. He believed that the constant threat of persecution under which the early churches laboured, was not unlike the constant threat of annihilation under which the wartime Londoners lived. After youth club activities Phillips would read a few verses from Paul's letters; 'After all, I thought to myself, much of this was written by one Christian in difficulty to other Christians in difficulty, and surely these young people will find them appropriate to their situation.' But Phillips was disappointed; 'I was met by polite but complete lack of comprehension. These youngsters, who were by no means unintelligent, simply did not understand Bible language.'[4]

Phillips had been a brilliant scholar at Cambridge and had an excellent grasp of Greek. Throughout his ministry he had had a 'passion for making truth comprehensible'. He had also developed an enviable ability to communicate with all age and social groups in a form of English that was both intelligible and compelling. He was familiar with the other modern translations undertaken in the twentieth century and quietly deplored the stuffy, 'translators' English' in which they were written.

In his busy wartime schedule Dr. Phillips set aside one morning each week for translating Paul's letters. When he had completed the letter to the Colossians he sent a copy to C. S. Lewis of Magdalen College, Oxford. He received his reply on 3 August 1943. Lewis wrote: 'Thank you a hundred times. I thought I knew Colossians pretty well, but your paraphrase made it far more significant — it was like seeing a familiar picture after it's been cleaned.' Lewis encouraged Phillips to complete all of Paul's letters and to publish them under the title of *Letters to Young Churches*. As he worked on his translation Phillips tried it out on his youth groups and found an instant and positive response. *Letters to Young Churches* was finally published in 1947 with a preface written by C. S. Lewis. It was an immediate success. Within a short time J. B. Phillips was being interviewed on both radio and television. In no time his fame had spread across the Atlantic. In 1952 he published *The Gospels in Modern English*.

Of *Letters to Young Churches* Professor F. F. Bruce wrote: 'Undoubtedly, of all modern English translations of the New Testament epistles, this is one of the best — perhaps actually *the* best — for the ordinary reader.'[5]

There can be little doubt that it was the early success of J. B. Phillips that ignited the enthusiasm in the established churches of England and Scotland to produce a completely new translation of the English Bible. The general assembly of the Church of Scotland adopted the motion in 1946. They then approached the Church of England and the principal free churches, and gradually won the approval of each. The inevitable joint committee was established in 1947. Dr. C. H. Dodd was appointed convenor for the New Testament panel. Dodd tells us that each book, or part of a book, was at first entrusted to an individual translator, before the committee got to work on it. Dodd's expressed aim: 'It is to be genuinely English in idiom, such as will not awaken a sense of strangeness or remoteness. Ideally, we aim at timeless English, avoiding equally both archaisms and transient modernisms. The version should be plain enough to convey its meaning to any reasonably intelligent person . . . yet not bald or pedestrian.'

What resulted was the *New English Bible*. The New Testament appeared in 1961 and the complete Bible — one edition included the Apocrypha — appeared in 1970.

Of the 'hundreds of one-man versions of the whole or parts of the Bible into English made this century',[6] J. B. Phillips without question came nearest to the common man. In 1958 he published *The New Testament in Modern English*. Thereafter he worked hard on Hebrew and, by 1963, managed to publish translations of four prophetic books from the Old Testament under the title of *Four Prophets*. But Phillips was a popular broadcaster and communicator engaged in preparing radio programmes and writing easy-to-read paperbacks. He did not persist with the Old Testament. Instead he returned to the New. In 1972 he published a revised edition of *The New Testament in Modern English* in which he incorporated more than 2,000 changes. Phillips continues to emerge 'top of the pile' when scholars 'compare and contrast' what the modern versions have to offer.[7]

For some, however, three modern versions which emerged out of America in the 1970s and 1980s have eclipsed Phillips. Certainly the popular paraphrase, *The Living Bible*, first published in 1971, rivals Phillips for readability. While no translator can avoid paraphrasing, Dr. John Taylor in his introduction to his *Living Bible* emphasizes that it is purely and simply a paraphrase. His original aim was to write a Bible that would be interesting to and understood by his own children.

The aim of Phillips to avoid theological terms and pious phraseology was taken over by the translators of the *Good News Bible*, another version (translation) that rivals Phillips for readability. It was published by the American Bible Society and Collins.

The *New International Version*, translated by a group of conservative, evangelical scholars and published by the New York Bible Society, rivals Phillips in combining modernity and accuracy of translation. First published in 1977 it is beginning to appear as a kind of 'new authorised version' among evangelical Nonconformists.

Increasingly, for scholars, preachers and ordinary readers,

The Revised English Bible published in 1989 by Oxford and Cambridge combines the best of all worlds. It began as a revision of the *New English Bible* but, as the translators had recourse to the Hebrew and Greek manuscripts and involved contemporary writers in their work, it emerged as a totally new translation. It is felt that it combines the best in modern English with the highest standards of accuracy in translation.

But the reverence for the King James Bible is still very much alive, especially among fundamentalist Christians. In 1982 a 'Revised Authorised Version' of the King James Bible — retaining the grandeur of its language but removing its inaccuracies — was published in the United States.

Many are confused by the sheer number of different translations now available and ask the question, 'Which version is best?' The response to this question has to be, 'Best — for what?'

The only way to find out which version is best for you is to visit a library or bookshop, take the various versions off the shelves — and sample them.

Do any of the versions contain theological bias? After a lifetime of research and comparison, immersed in the Greek in which the New Testament is written, Dr. A. Graham Maxwell has said: 'I've gone through every version looking for signs of theological bias, and have found it so rare as to be conspicuous.' Times have changed since the age of Tyndale and Coverdale. The Bible translators, insists Maxwell, have been very honest men; all versions come ultimately from the same Hebrew, Aramaic and Greek. 'And that's where the great safety lies. The scholars are constantly watching one another.'

English is the most Bible-rich language on earth.

References
[1] F. F. Bruce, *The English Bible* (1961), page 128.
[2] The most important variants are dealt with above in the chapter entitled, 'The Find of a Life-time'.

[3] A. M. Hunter, *Interpreting the New Testament 1900-1950*, (1951).
[4] J. B. Phillips, *The Price of Success: An Autobiography* (1984), pages 99, 100.
[5] F. F. Bruce *op cit*, page 214.
[6] Pearl Sjolander, *Some Aspects of Style in Twentieth-century English Bible Translation* (1979), page 9.
[7] Robert Bratcher cited ibid, page 49.

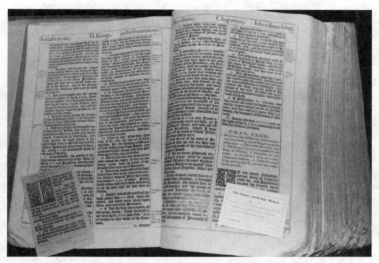

A first edition of the King James Bible (1611) found in the William Cowper - John Newton Museum, Olney, Buckinghamshire.

The Rosetta Stone was discovered during Napoleon's Egyptian
campaign, 1798. It contains the record of a royal decree
written in three languages: hieroglyphs (top); demotic script
(middle); and Greek (bottom). By making it possible for
scholars to understand hieroglyphs it unlocked the treasure
house of Egyptian history written on tombs and temples.

ARCHAEOLOGY
AND THE
BIBLE

Wanted! A key to the ancient world

The lands of the Middle and Near East had been a magnet for pilgrims from the third century.

Pie-eyed, they looked at the pyramids, the ruined temples, the long-deserted, crumbled-down cities. Egypt in particular had a wealth of 'pictures' carved out of stone walls, preserved for thousands of years. And generations of ancient scribes had chiselled out the story of their times on the self-same stone walls, and on tablets dug out on occasion from warm sands. But what did it all mean? It was assumed that no one would ever know. Great civilizations in the millennia before Christ had left their artefacts, great nations their stories in stone, great dynasties depositions of their deeds. But they were unread and, it was assumed, unreadable.

For some this made them all the more intriguing. During the eighteenth century, driven by demand from the West for the treasures of long-dead civilizations in the East, some adventurers with an eye on the cash prize began to rummage.

They rummaged in Italy and Greece and Turkey. The really adventurous rummaged further afield; Syria, Palestine, Mesopotamia. The exciting 'discoveries' they stumbled into — among them, the cities of Baalbek, Palmyra and Petra — whetted the appetites of men of a more scholarly turn of mind.

Those who rummaged in Egypt had the most rewarding time. But they could not understand what they saw. Their fantastic accounts of pyramids and temples and painted tombs were no more than travellers' tales.

So much to be seen; but who could understand it? So much to be found; but who could interpret its significance? So many treasures; but who knew enough to appreciate their value?

Wanted. A key to unlock the door to the ancient world. Most doubted that such a key existed.

Placing implicit faith in their doubts, eighteenth century Enlightenment scholars decided it was time to debunk the Bible for good and all. Their argument went something like this:

As history, the Old Testament was totally unreliable. Abraham and his family had not begun the patriarchal line; they had lived at the time of the kings of Israel — or even later! The so-called 'laws of Moses' had nothing whatever to do with Moses, but had been written by priests at the time of the Exile! Indeed, doubt was cast as to whether or not Moses would actually have been able to write! And as to the nation of the Hittites which loomed so large in Old Testament historical narratives, this was a mythical race, it had never existed: there was consensus on this point. The Assyrian and Babylonian kings whose names and doings peppered the Old Testament, the odd one might have existed, but most were the invention of the ever-fecund Hebrew imagination. . . .

The 'experts' were guilty of bad timing as well as misinformation. No sooner had they debunked the Bible to their mutual satisfaction than the first of the elusive keys was discovered. . . .

The Rosetta Stone

The Rosetta Stone was the key to the secrets of ancient Egypt which, in turn, shed considerable light on the history of other nations — and on the Bible narrative.

When Napoleon invaded Egypt in 1798 his military aim was to use it as a spring-board to India. As a military venture his Egyptian campaign was a failure. As part of the story of the Bible it must be counted a great success.

Napoleon had brought with him to Egypt 175 French scholars. Like many of his contemporaries, Napoleon was acutely aware of Egypt as a treasure-house of the past. Before beginning to fight the Battle of the Pyramids, looking around, he announced to his commanders: 'Forty centuries look down upon you!'

Napoleon's scholars mapped Egypt in detail. While some made maps others went in search of Egyptian carvings and other treasures which could be transported back to France. Near Rosetta on the Nile a fascinating stone was found. Much later it was discovered to contain the record of a decree of King Ptolemy V in three languages: hieroglyphs (top); demotic script (middle); and Greek (bottom).

While Napoleon's armies were fighting inland his battleships and transport vessels were destroyed by Admiral Nelson at the Battle of the Nile. Eventually Napoleon deserted his army and took ship back to France. His scholars were left to make what arrangements they could with what they had found. The ships they chartered, loaded with ancient artefacts including the Rosetta Stone, were intercepted by the British fleet on their way back to France. Most of the booty found its way to the British Museum where it still is.

Recognizing the first language of the stone to be hieroglyphs and very much aware that the inscriptions on the tombs and temples of Egypt were written in hieroglyphs, the French scholars had taken a plaster cast of the Rosetta Stone. Hence, in the years after the Egyptian campaign, scholars in both London and Paris were studying the three languages of the Rosetta Stone.

Reading the Greek was easy. Once they had established that the identical decree was being given in all three languages, the demotic script was also deciphered. The really difficult part, however, was making sense of the hieroglyphic script.

Jean-Francois Champollion takes the principal credit for deciphering Egyptian hieroglyphics. Having pored over many hieroglyphic inscriptions in different parts of Egypt he became fascinated by the first language of the Rosetta Stone. Making sense of it became an obsession with him. In 1822 he realized something of vital importance: the hieroglyphs were not simply symbols or letters — they represented sounds, and whole words. *Within a few days he had broken this most difficult of scripts and, in doing so, unlocked the history of a nation that cut a swathe right through the history of the Old Testament and beyond.*

The ancient monuments of Egypt were covered with hieroglyphics which had remained dumb for 2,000 years. Now they were made to speak.

As exponents of the new-born science of archaeology converged on Egypt to read the record of its past, they were well aware that archaeology could not 'prove' or 'disprove' God or whether God spoke through Moses or Isaiah or any of the other Bible prophets. However, they also knew that if they could find evidence of the existence of particular individuals or nations whose existence had been denied by the 'experts', and if they could ascertain that the chronology of the Bible narrative — denied by 'experts' — was in fact accurate, they were in a position to give the lie to the 'debunking' school of thought. Or, at least, to introduce a little humility into some of its pronouncements. . . .

The Behistun Rock

The understanding of Egyptian hieroglyphics represented just one key to unlock the ancient world.

Another form of writing used in most parts of the Middle East was termed *cuneiform.*

Cuneiform means 'wedge-shaped'. It was a name invented

for a certain type of writing by French and English archaeologists, and derives from the Latin. It has become clear that cuneiform was used widely in the Eastern world for over 3,000 years.

It was developed by the original Sumerian inhabitants of Babylonia. It was commonplace at the beginning of the patriarchal period. Abraham's departure from Ur is believed to have taken place about the time of Hammurabi (*circa* 1850 BC). One thousand years before Hammurabi chiselled his code of laws on a slab of stone, the Sumerians had begun to use cuneiform.

In the early years of archaeological excavation clay tablets containing cuneiform script were being found throughout the Middle East. They fascinated the scholars. It was clear to them that cuneiform had developed out of the same kind of pictorial script as hieroglyphics. In Babylonia, however, the almost complete absence of stone had compelled the scribe to make use of clay. At first attempts had been made to draw pictures upon the clay. Soon, however, the scribe had found it more convenient just to press the edge of his square-ended stick or stylus into the soft clay and so to build up his characters, not by outline, but by a series of triangular or wedge-shaped characters.

Cuneiform was found in Egypt, but it is clear that it did not displace hieroglyphics. Abraham would have encountered it in Ur, and may have encountered it in Egypt. It would have accompanied him all along the trade route north-west of Syria, then south-west through Canaan. Centuries later a man like Moses 'learned in all the wisdom of the Egyptians' would have been able to read and reproduce both hieroglyphics and cuneiform. The Tell el Amarna Tablets, written close to the Mosaic era, indicate that even Canaanite-speaking people could produce cuneiform. Hence it is clear that throughout the patriarchal period Bible characters are likely to have been

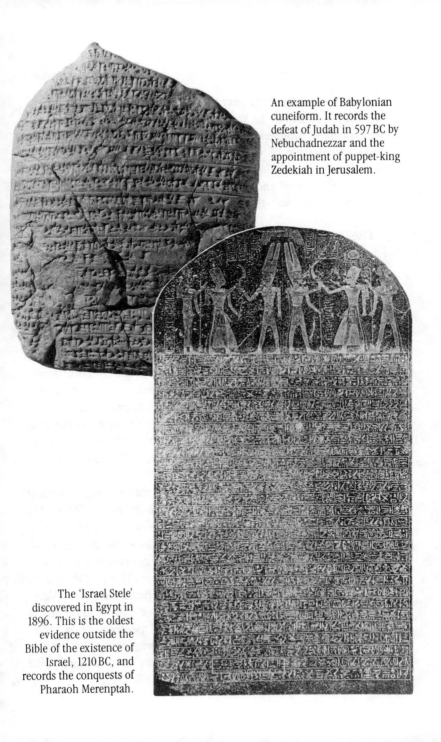

An example of Babylonian cuneiform. It records the defeat of Judah in 597 BC by Nebuchadnezzar and the appointment of puppet-king Zedekiah in Jerusalem.

The 'Israel Stele' discovered in Egypt in 1896. This is the oldest evidence outside the Bible of the existence of Israel, 1210 BC, and records the conquests of Pharaoh Merenptah.

literate. In the light of recent research, far from questioning the ability of Moses to write, it may even be conjectured that he may have progressed beyond clumsy syllabic scripts to an alphabetical style of writing, not dissimilar from the Hebrew of a later age.

Making sense of the different variations in cuneiform script was the second key that unlocked the history of the ancient world.

The story of how cuneiform was finally 'cracked' by the scholars is inextricably tied up with the Behistun Rock.

For centuries travellers between Tehran and Baghdad had had to pass by the massive rock face at Behistun. They had looked up and seen, 300 feet above road level, a detailed carving. A number of men figured in the carving, and a large area surrounding it had been rendered smooth.

Over the years climbers had ventured up to take a closer look. They had noticed marks cut into the smooth stone. Drawings were made of the marks and scholars puzzled over the drawings — but made no sense of them.

Carsten Niebuhr, an expert in Arabic, was perhaps the first to make an attempt to decipher what was clearly writing of some sort. He saw that there were three different kinds of script.

George Grotefend, a German school master, was the next to attempt to decipher the script on the Behistun Rock. He actually identified the names of Darius and Xerxes. But it was to take a great many more years before the Behistun inscriptions were the means of deciphering Persian cuneiform. It was to be the achievement of Englishman Henry Rawlinson.

In 1836 Rawlinson began work on the Behistun texts. Working in intense heat at the top of a ladder cannot have made things easy. At times he found himself perched on a ledge only eighteen inches wide. In 1837 he completed a translation of 200 lines. From his transcription Persian cuneiform had been deciphered within ten years.

Rawlinson had identified other types of cuneiform writing on the cliff face at Behistun. One of them incorporated over 100 signs, too many to be an alphabet. Only long years of study and assistance from experts employed by the Royal Asiatic Society, enabled him to decipher Susian or Elamite cuneiform. This had been done by 1855.

But as with the Rosetta Stone, there were actually *three* languages on the Behistun Rock. Rawlinson now turned his attention to the third. This time he had the indispensable help of an Anglican clergyman, Edward Hincks, and a Kurdish boy who risked life and limb on a daily basis to take impressions from inaccessible parts of the rock face. The language turned out to be Assyrian or Babylonian cuneiform. It was identified and deciphered in 1857.

As a key to the past the third language of Behistun was to be more important than the rest. For 2,500 years the records of Assyria and Babylonia had been silent. Now, thanks to Rawlinson and his helpers, they could speak.

The Old Testament contained a tremendous amount of detailed information about both Assyria and Babylonia. Now that Babylonian cuneiform had been deciphered, archaeologists were keen to discover whether it was fact or fiction. . . .

Treasure Tells

The third key to unlock the world of the Bible was the Middle Eastern *tell*.

A tell is a flat-topped mound, without interest to the uninformed.

For modern archaeology it is fortunate that the tells *were* without interest for many centuries. A virgin tell is a city with its history intact waiting to be read by the archaeologist and his team. Its history may stretch back three, four, even five thousand years.

A tell is invariably found near a water source. In the mists of the past a collection of families would take a decision to build a community, often in a defensible position. Around their community or settlement they would build ramparts of mud or brick.

With the passage of centuries their town would be destroyed by enemies. They would then rebuild on the same site (for the same reasons that the settlement was established there in the first place), building over the ruins of the first settlement. Depending upon the scale of destruction there might be long periods in which the settlement might be left abandoned. In that event the rain, driven by the prevailing west wind, would wash the debris of house walls and roofs off the site until further erosion was checked by the arrival of another collection of families and the rebuilding of fortifications and dwellings.

As successive occupations would follow one upon another a tell would gradually develop. Each occupation would be marked by its own stratum, like the layers of a cake. With each new settlement the area of development would decrease slightly and the town be built further from ground level. Eventually the tell would reach a considerable height. For example, the tell of Beth-Shan is seventy feet high.

The number of strata varies from one tell to another. The area of a tell varies from between 2.5 acres to 13 acres. The tell of Hazor north of Galilee is 100 acres.

Each stratum will contain, not just masonry, but pottery of various kinds. The profusion of pottery in Middle Eastern tells enabled archaeologists to date each stratum even prior to the use of carbon-14 dating. Amulets are found frequently. A *stele* (tablet) covered with hieroglyphs or a cylinder-seal or cuneiform tablet are a real find.

At first archaeologists simply worked 'downwards'. They began with the topmost stratum, clearing away the loose debris until walls, rooms and artefacts emerged. When a stratum was finished with, the walls were simply removed — and the next stratum tackled. This 'working downwards' method is known to archaeologists as the Reisner-Fisher technique.

In 1952-58 Dame Kathleen Kenyon applied Sir Mortimer Wheeler's trenching method on Jericho. The results were so brilliant that trenching has become standard practice. Before excavation a trench is dug through *all* the layers of the mound. This is now known as the Wheeler-Kenyon technique. It supplemented but did not displace the Reisner-Fisher technique. The careful use of test trenches helps to determine exact stratification before digging an area; followed by additional test trenches at right-angles to walls as they are cleared.

When an excavation is completed the material is prepared for publication; everything meticulously recorded, drawn and photographed.

The discovery of the nature of the tell and the development of the various techniques to interpret its contents has provided a vast amount of information about the cities mentioned in Bible times. Babylon, Ninevah, Susa, Ur, Jericho, Megiddo, Samaria and Hazor are just a few of the Bible cities which, having been silent for centuries, have yielded their secrets to the archaeologist's spade. Not only have they provided valuable background colour to life in Old Testament times, but their cuneiform-covered *steles* have authenticated matters of detail.

The doors to the ancient world have been unlocked. We can peer back down the ages — watch the armies of Caesar, Alexander, Cyrus and Sennacherib. In the distance we can see patriarchs and pharaohs, prophets and kings. Then, as the evidence of the spade confirms the book time after time we experience exhilaration, and more. Much more. For the Bible is far more than the most detailed, accurate ancient history book. . . .

The great empires of the East

By 1865 the door to the World of the Bible with its treasures and its secrets was open.

The ancient languages had been deciphered. The inscriptions were yielding their mysteries.

When the realization — at the same time — that a tell represented accumulations of layers of occupation, the great age of biblical archaeology was under starter's orders.

In Britain, France, Germany and the United States funds were set up to finance the work of this new breed of scientist: the archaeologist.

Soon archaeological finds were front-page news in Western newspapers.

The names of Egyptian pharaohs, dead for three-and-a-half millennia, became household words. Discussion began: Who was the pharaoh who enslaved the Israelites? Who was the pharaoh at the time of the Exodus? *When* was the Exodus?

The Assyrian tyrants mentioned in Scripture were found carved on their palace walls, with their armies and their miserable captives.

The great kings of Persia began to speak through their writings.

As the tells of Palestine and Iraq were excavated evidence was found which corroborated and added colour to the Bible record.

The history books of the Old Testament came alive!

Sir Henry Layard, Hormuz Rassam and Paul Emile Botta

discovered the long-forgotten sites of Nineveh and Babylon.

Babylon: City of gold

For centuries Babylon had been the key metropolis of Mesopotamia — the land between the Tigris and Euphrates rivers, now called Iraq. It flourished for nearly 2,000 years until its capture by Alexander the Great in 331 BC. Famous kings like Hammurabi and Nebuchadnezzar presided over the days of its glory. The Greeks remembered it as containing *two* of the seven wonders of the ancient world.

At the height of Babylon's splendour, Hebrew prophet Isaiah described it as *'the glory of kingdoms, the splendour and pride of the Chaldeans'* (Isaiah 13:19, RSV). More surprisingly Isaiah went on to say that Babylon would *'be like Sodom and Gomorrah when God overthrew them. It will never be inhabited or dwelt in for all generations; no Arab will pitch his tent there, no shepherds will make their flocks lie down there. But wild beasts will lie down there, and its houses will be full of howling creatures.'* (Isaiah 13:19-21, RSV.)

In 1807 Claudius Rich — who could read Arabic, Syriac, Hebrew and Persian — became the East India Company's representative in Baghdad. In 1811, accompanied by his teenage bride, he made his first excursion to Babylon. He set men to dig for inscribed tablets, seals and sculpted walls. His report and sketches, published as *Memoir of the Ruins of Babylon*, described the scene Isaiah had foretold.

Though the place was pure wilderness it continued to fascinate scholars because of its importance in Old Testament history and New Testament imagery. Major excavations began in 1899. The archaeologist Robert Koldewey received generous sponsorship from Imperial Germany. City walls, temples, palaces and houses were uncovered. Scores of basketsful of pottery and cartloads of stone carvings with cuneiform inscriptions were removed for study. Almost all dated from the period

626-539 BC: *the reign of Nebuchadnezzar*. Accounts were discovered of Nebuchadnezzar's victorious campaigns against the Assyrians and Egyptians, *and of his annexation of Judah*. Babylonian inscriptions dovetailed with the biblical narrative.

From the discoveries in Babylon it has been possible to reconstruct the glory of this once massively beautiful city with its hanging gardens. Fascinating artefacts are to be found in the British Museum and the State Museum in Berlin. However, aside from an artist's reconstruction of the Ishtar Gate, nothing now stands on the site. It is still rubbled over. The site of the great ziggurat was scraped clear by Alexander. He died before he could rebuild it. It remains just as he left it. At night jackals and hyenas make their noises, and their noises, echoing among the ruins, disturb flocks of sheep nearby. Other great cities of the ancient world — Jerusalem, Damascus, Athens, Rome — have been destroyed and rebuilt. Not Babylon. The prophet was right.

The Greek historian Herodotus says that the Babylonian king overlaid the walls of his great temple with gold, providing a great gold-plated bed and throne for his god. Two gold statues of Marduk were there, one sitting, one standing. Twenty tons of gold were used for the temple and its furniture. '*You are this head of gold*,' Daniel told Nebuchadnezzar when he expounded the image-vision. (Daniel 2:38.) Nebuchadnezzar would have latched on immediately. His was a *city* of gold.

A great processional way divided Babylon in half. Inscribed on paving stones and bricks was this legend: 'I am Nebuchadnezzar, king of Babylon, son of Nabopolassar, king of Babylon.' Nebuchadnezzar wanted present and posterity to know to whose glory this magnificent city was built. His claim is reflected in the pages of Scripture; ' "*Is not this great Babylon which I have built . . . ?*" ' (Daniel 4:30, RSV.)

His achievement was great; but in the perspective of history his boast rings hollow. Not only had his city remained a scene of desolation for thousands of years, but biblical critics had been laughing off Nebuchadnezzar — and his grandson, Belshazzar — as figures of myth and folklore.

Until Koldewey's discoveries, that is, obliged them to be silent.

The long road to Nineveh

Claudius Rich had had no difficulty identifying Babylon. The ruined mound in Lower Mesopotamia was still called Tell Babil. And the scientific archaeologists who took up his work seventy years after he died of cholera, never questioned his identification. There was ample evidence.

But what of Nineveh, capital of the mighty Assyrian Empire? Nineveh, whose might had to be brought down to make way for Babylon?

The site of Nineveh appeared to have been completely lost.

In 1836 someone published Rich's records. He had, it appeared, explored a site near Mosul called Tell Nebi Yunus — The Mound of the Prophet Jonah. From Jonah's association with Ninevah the pre-archaeologists leapt to the conclusion that the twin mounds of Tell Nebi Yunus and Kuyunjik, on the Tigris river opposite to modern Mosul, marked the site of the ancient Assyrian capital.

Paul Emile Botta, with financial backing from the French government, began excavations of a sort in 1842. But before cuneiform had been deciphered he was working in the dark, unable to assess the significance of his discoveries.

While Botta's army of diggers was at work, a man from the village of *Khorsabad* who regularly passed their excavations began to take an interest. If it was inscriptions and sculptures they were after, he told them, then they could do worse than visit *Khorsabad*. His home village was actually built on top of a mound (tell) and people were constantly coming across inscribed limestone slabs.

Botta sent a couple of his senior men to check out the suggestion. Within minutes of their arrival at *Khorsabad* they unearthed a number of large, beautifully-carved slabs of stone. Within a month Botta had transferred his entire party to this new tell.

The work on *Khorsabad* began in 1843. Within two years Botta's discoveries were hogging the headlines. The vast palace of an Assyrian king was excavated. *Which* Assyrian king, they did not know, since they could not read the cuneiform inscriptions. But Botta was sure it was Nineveh. This is what he told the world. For a considerable period he was believed; what other city could yield such huge bas-reliefs — vast winged and human-headed lions and bulls, inscriptions galore, as well as *objects d'art* and weapons of war?

Only after Sir Henry Rawlinson had completely deciphered the Behistun inscription was it possible to say for sure that Botta was wrong.

But Botta had made huge collections of inscriptions. Rawlinson and his students were now able to ascertain what Botta *had* found.

The identity of the city under *Khorsabad* and the palace it contained were soon known. The palace had been that of Sargon II, Sennacherib's father. Sargon, Botta was told, was the conqueror of Samaria, capital of the Northern Kingdom of Israel. And he had left a detailed account of his conquest in cuneiform: 'I besieged and conquered Samaria and led away as booty 27,290 inhabitants of it.' What Sargon does *not* explain is that he was a general working under Shalmaneser V (see 2 Kings 18) at the time of the three campaigns against Samaria. Hence, in *his* annals, Shalmaneser claims to have conquered Samaria too!

The discovery of all this was a black eye for those sceptical of Bible accuracy. Until these discoveries the names Sargon and Shalmaneser — like Nebuchadnezzar and Belshazzar —

had not existed outside the Bible (Isaiah 20:1). 'Mythical characters', the sceptics had said. Botta may not have found Nineveh, but he had 'found Sargon' and Sargon's palace, together with a detailed record of conquests which corroborated the biblical account. And soon he had 'found Shalmaneser' too!

From Botta's finds, Rawlinson drew the first reference to a king of Israel. Israel was referred to as 'the land of Omri'. Omri was the founder of a strong dynasty which included Ahab, and was the northern king responsible for moving the capital to Samaria.

Khorsabad was not built over Ninevah, but over a veritable treasure-house of archaeological finds that has still to be exhausted. Sargon's palace with its gigantic winged bulls has now been completely excavated. On its walls are reliefs of battles, scenes of pomp and splendour, together with a comprehensive list of the kings of Assyria (indispensable to the archaeologist).

The search for Nineveh had proved fruitful in terms of biblical archaeology. But where *was* Nineveh, *'that great city', 'pride of the Assyrians'*?

Englishman Henry Layard had been pursuing yet another dead-end road to Nineveh. Instead he had found *Nimrud*, a city built by Nimrod and known to Scripture as *Calah* (Genesis 10:11).

Again it was Rawlinson's 'decoding' of the cuneiform that disabused the hopeful explorer. Layard was compensated, to some extent, by the discovery among the debris of centuries, of a giant monument which, in the face of the disapproval of the Turkish authorities, he shipped to the British Museum. Here it now resides in splendour: a great winged, human-headed lion. Another pointer to the brilliance of the empire of which Nineveh was the capital.

This was only one exciting discovery at *Nimrud*.

Layard uncovered the Black Obelisk of Shalmaneser III (now in the British Museum). Carved into the hard black stone are five sections of reliefs and inscriptions. With Rawlinson's help, another reference to a Hebrew king was found; 'Jehu the son of Omri.' The adjacent relief depicted Jehu, among other subject kings, paying tribute to an Assyrian official.

As Layard's diggers worked on at *Nimrud*, the ruins of the palaces, large dwelling houses and administrative buildings of a prosperous city were laid bare. Winged animals, distinctive of Assyrian sculpture, lined the walls. After Layard's time monuments to the great Assyrian kings were discovered, together with a large number of carved ivory plaques. This ivory aroused much interest.

The biblical record refers to Ahab's palace *'inlaid with ivory'* (1 Kings 22:39, NIV). Archaeologists have made the assumption that the ivory found in the palace at *Nimrud* may well have been part of the loot brought from Samaria after its fall. During Dame Kathleen Kenyon's excavation of Samaria, in more recent times, ivory objects were found identical to those discovered years before at *Nimrud* in Iraq.

In 1989 *Nimrud* yielded more treasures, including a vast wealth of jewellery and the tomb of Yabahya, daughter of Saragon II.

But where was Nineveh? Why was it proving so elusive? At first Layard held to the view that *Nimrud* was Nineveh. But the cuneiform tablets made this contention impossible to maintain.

It was the decipherment of cuneiform script that enabled scholars to plot the location of Nineveh. It lay opposite present-day Mosul. Botta had been mistaken in being lured away from the twin mounds of *Kuyunjik* and *Nebi Yunus* to the treasure-house at *Khorsabad*. Under the twin mounds were the old palaces and temples of Ninevah.

The presence of an Islamic sacred place on the top of *Nebi Yunus* has made excavation difficult there. Hence most of the information we have about Nineveh comes from work done on the mound of *Kuyunjik.*

Here a discovery of the greatest importance was made: the Library of Ashurbanipal. Literally tens of thousands of cuneiform documents, some historical, some literary, gave an insight into a rich and lavish civilization.

At last Nineveh had been discovered. And what a discovery! In 1854, throughout the civilized world, newspapers carried the story that Rassam had found at Nineveh an ancient Babylonian legend of creation strongly reminiscent of the book of Genesis: The Gilgamesh Epic. Nineveh again hit the headlines in 1871 when George Smith, a journalist employed by the *Daily Telegraph,* discovered the Gilgamesh Flood Epic which also paralleled the flood story in Genesis.

On the tablets in the Library of Ashurbanipal, Nineveh, were found the names of a variety of Bible characters including Ahab, Hezekiah, Sennacherib, Sargon and many others.

Work on Nineveh continues. Elongated mounds, the remnants of old fortification walls, are still being discovered. It has been asserted that the total length of one of these walls is no less than seven-and-a-half miles; in short, Nineveh went far beyond the twin mounds of *Kuyunjik* and *Nebi Yunus.* The greater part of Nineveh is now covered with fields. With difficulty two gates have been excavated and partly restored. A royal palace has been excavated. But, to the modern visitor, Nineveh comes as a disappointment. 'There is nothing to see,' they say. 'Just endless flat land with the occasional rubbish heap!'

If Nineveh is an anti-climax it is also a fulfilment of prophecy. At the height of Babylon's power Isaiah prophesied its total destruction. At the height of the power of Assyria's cruel capital, the Hebrew prophet Nahum prophesied the destruction of an empire which, in his day, stretched from the Black Sea in the north to the frontiers of Ethiopia in the south. From the sands of Arabia to the shores of the Mediterranean and on to the bleak northlands of Persia. For centuries Assyria was unassailable, a military juggernaut crushing all beneath it. But, projected forward in time, Nahum saw a scene like this: *'Woe to the city of blood, full of lies, full of plunder, never without victims!*

The crack of whips, the clatter of wheels, galloping horses and jolting chariots!

Charging cavalry, flashing swords and glittering spears!

Many casualties, piles of dead, bodies without number, people stumbling over the corpses . . .

"I am against you," declares the Lord Almighty . . .

"I will show the nations your nakedness and the kingdoms your shame. . . . I will treat you with contempt and make you a spectacle. All who see you will flee from you and say, 'Ninevah is in ruins — who will mourn for her?' " . . . Nothing can heal your wound; your injury is fatal. Everyone who hears the news about you claps his hands at your fall, for who has not felt your endless cruelty?' (Nahum 3:1-3, 5-7, 19, NIV.)

The biblical record indicates that, at the height of its power, Nineveh had a population of 120,000 (Jonah 4:11). Making a comparison between the area ancient Nineveh occupied, with that covered by modern Mosul, which has a population of 100,000, the biblical figures are certainly realistic. Nineveh's prophet began preaching after walking *'a day's journey'* into the city (Jonah 3:4). It was said that *'Nineveh was an exceeding great city of three days' journey'* (Jonah 3:3).

On the seven-and-a-half mile wall and detailed, painstaking excavation of the vast area of rubbled terrain are present-day indicators of the enormous scale of this once vast metropolis.

In 612 BC Nineveh fell to the combined might of the Medes and the Babylonians. The fortifications were demolished and the palaces and temples were razed. The greater part of the population was slaughtered without mercy.

Two hundred years after the fall of Nineveh, Greek historian and military leader Xenophon, with an army of 10,000, marched along the Tigris river after the Battle of Kunaxa. He caught sight of the landscape littered with heaps of ruins that had once been Nineveh. Xenophon asked the name of this great city of old. Those living near the site tendered their most humble apologies to the great general. The name of this city, they said, had been completely forgotten.

18

What happened to the Hittites?

Samaria was under siege from the Syrians. The hordes of Damascus had the capital of the Northern Kingdom at their mercy. Massive carnage was expected.

Then, overnight, a rumour spread through the Syrian camp. The King of Israel, it was said, had made an alliance with the King of the Hittites. This caused such terror among the Syrian army that they fled and the siege came to an unaccountable end. (2 Kings 7.)

This is just one of the Old Testament references to a powerful people called the Hittites. From the Old Testament context it is clear that the Hittites represented one of the super-powers over a period of many centuries. It is equally clear that individual Hittite families were permitted to live at peace in the Israelite kingdoms and that Hittite commanders held positions of honour close to Israelite kings.

In the eighteenth and nineteenth centuries the Hittites were a source of considerable embarrassment to both Christian and Jewish scholars. Despite the high profile of the Hittites in the Old Testament, there was no reference to such a people anywhere else. On no subject did the scholars intent on discrediting the biblical record render themselves more insufferable. 'The Hittites? Who were the Hittites? There were no such people as the Hittites! The Hittites were never mentioned by classical historians. Therefore, there *were* no Hittites. The Bible must be untrue. Just another example of a fabled people produced by a fecund imagination.'

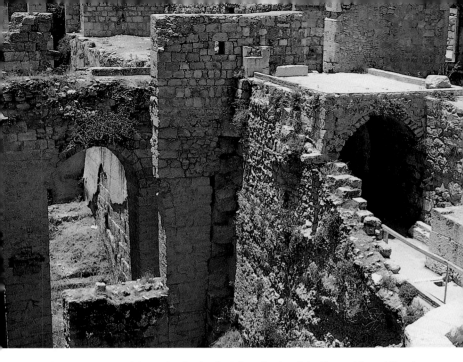

Above, excavations of the Pools of Bethesda. Below, the site of the First and Second Temples now dominated by the El Aksa mosque and the Dome of the Rock.

Above, St. Catherine's monastery, Sinai, where Constantin Tischendorf found the Codex Sinaiticus. Below, excavations now in progress in the area between Temple Mount and the City of David.

Above, the Muslim Dome of the Rock built, partially, over the area once covered by Herod the Great's Temple. Below, part of a scale model of Herod's Jerusalem. On the left of the picture, the Temple; on the right, part of the Antonia Fortress.

Above, the Western Wall, the lower part is all that is left of the platform Herod the Great constructed as a base for his enlarged Temple. Below, excavations of the synagogue of Capernaum, *circa* fourth century.

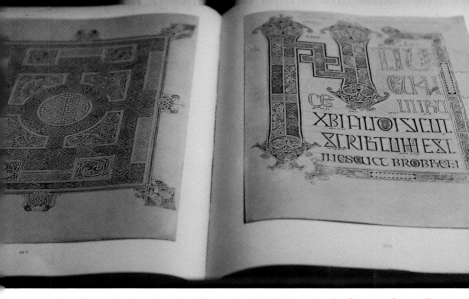

Above, the Lindisfarne Gospels, (now in the British Museum), the finest artefacts still remaining of the Celtic Church. Below, the Codex Sinaiticus, one of the fifty accurate copies of the Bible commissioned by Emperor Constantine in AD 331.

Aiden, champion of
Celtic Christianity, on
Lindisfarne.

Above, ruins of the Lindisfarne monastery. Below, Whitby Abbey which, thanks to Caedmon, played a part in the story of the English Bible.

A statue of Jerome (*c.* AD347-420) at Bethlehem (above). He translated the 'Latin Vulgate' from the 'Old Latin' version of *c.* AD150. Below, the Reformation Monument, Geneva. The Reformation was the great age of vernacular Bibles.

Once again the dogmatic critics were to end up with egg on their faces. So much egg, in fact, that if such bold assertions had been made in any other academic discipline than biblical criticism — and then been so conclusively confounded — there would have had to have been many resignations from important positions in the universities and in the churches. However, there is no record that any such resignations occurred when, to quote A. H. Sayce, 'All of a sudden we were digging up Hittites all over the place!'

In fact the rediscovery of the Hittites began in 1876. At first it was largely the work of English scholar A. H. Sayce. *En route* between his houseboat on the Nile and the University of Oxford where, each spring, Dr. Sayce gave a series of lectures, he passed through the Near East. At Hama and Aleppo in Syria he found picture-writing on stone blocks reused in medieval buildings. Passing on through Turkey he found the same kind of writing carved on rocks. In 1876 he made a positive connection between these writings, the Hittites of the Old Testament, and the *Kheta* named in Egyptian texts.

The *Kheta* were one of the 'great powers' of the history inscribed in ancient Egyptian stone. It had been a source of puzzlement for archaeologists for many years to know who the *Kheta* were. One *Kheta* king, for example, had made a treaty with Pharaoh Rameses II. It was clear from the account of this treaty that the pharaoh and the king had made the treaty as equals. Where could a nation be found as powerful as that of the Egyptians at the height of their supremacy?

From 1876 the scholarly world had their answer to this question. An answer that had its origins, at first, in those strange hieroglyphic inscriptions in Syria and Turkey.

A. H. Sayce and W. Wright successfully dated the Hittite inscriptions to the centuries between 1600 and 700 BC. However, not until 1947, as a result of the work of Bossert, was hieroglyphic Hittite fully understood. Bossert found bilingual inscriptions — and suddenly the history of the Hittites was available to be read.

Long before 1947, however, it was realized that the Hittites were, in fact, a major power. Between 1906 and 1912 the Hittite capital *Hattushash* — now called Boghazkoy — was excavated by Hugo Winckler. The site was one hundred miles due east of Ankara, Turkey. Much of the Hittite city was above ground and, for years, the local Turks had been selling clay tablets as souvenirs to foreign visitors.

In the course of his excavations Winckler was fortunate enough to stumble upon the archives of the Hittite royal family. The tablets were written in cuneiform Hittite, a script used by the Hittites in addition to their hieroglyphic system of writing. Because of its similarity to Babylonian cuneiform, Hittite cuneiform was deciphered as early as 1915 by Czech scholar Hrozny. Ten thousand tablets containing cuneiform Hittite were found in the royal archives at *Hattushash*. Fascinating for those already aware of the treaty with Rameses II, was the discovery of the Hittite copy of the same treaty!

From the tablets of the royal archives emerged a chronology of Middle Eastern history, and the role played by the Hittites in it, during the period 1400-1200 BC. In addition there was a complete record of the Hittite kings during this period. It was clear that the Hittites were a civilized people and that their scribes were capable of writing in seven different languages (variants of cuneiform).

The excavation of the Hittite capital *Hattushash* was completed during the 1950s. It was a city of 300 acres. It was a well-constructed city of stone and brick, with more or less impregnable defences. On its east side was a high rock which had served as a fortified citadel. Within the city area five temples were uncovered. In the royal archives details had already been deciphered of the worship rituals of the Hittites, much being made in learned journals of their elaborate and lengthy religious services.

These details of a heathen system of worship, in themselves, were of considerable interest. The critics had previously claimed the Hebrew laws of Exodus, Leviticus, Numbers and Deuteronomy were too 'advanced' (complicated) to be dated to Moses' time. The *Hattushash* Tablets, together with tablets excavated in other Hittite cities, revealed a heathen system of worship equally as complex as that of Israel under Moses.

The symbol of the Hittites was the lion. Great lions stood on either side of the gateway to *Hattushash*.

Hittite cities and satellite states in northern Syria came to light. These were the cities with which Solomon had traded. (1 Kings 10:29.) Among them were *Zenjirli* and *Carchemish*.

It has been ascertained that the rise of the Hittites to major power status began in 1750 BC and that, although they continued to have significant political and cultural influence beyond that date, the sun had effectively set on the Hittite empire by about 1200 BC.

The *Encyclopaedia Britannica* devoted only eight lines to the Hittites in the 1860 edition. The 1947 edition of the same encyclopaedia was obliged to devote over ten full pages of two columns each to an article dealing with Hittite history, culture, and religion.

Evidently the Hittites were not one of the Bible's 'historical mistakes'. . . .

In search of the Hebrews

Creation and the Flood

The discovery at Ninevah of the Gilgamesh Epics turned the attention of Bible scholars to the early chapters of Genesis. The Creation Epic (discovered in 1854) and the Flood Epic (discovered in 1871) closely paralleled the Bible accounts.

There was a conscious search for other cuneiform accounts of the Creation and the Flood. In 1915 the oldest of all the Creation epics was found. This six-column *stele*, known as the Sumerian Epic, was dated to around 2350 BC, (the original form of the story may have pre-dated 3000 BC). It mirrored the Genesis account of creation to a surprising degree.

Babylonian accounts of the Deluge were discovered. They even contained the names of kings and dynasties which reigned *before* the Flood. The most interesting of these was the Blundell Prism.

Similarities notwithstanding, these other accounts of Creation and the Flood are uniformly inferior to the Hebrew account in Genesis. Inferior from a spiritual and moral, as well as a literary standpoint.

Sir Leonard Woolley's discovery of 'the empty stratum' during excavation in Mesopotamia during the 1920s was hailed as 'evidence of the flood'. It was, however, merely evidence of *a* flood; a widespread flood in the region between the Tigris and Euphrates rivers.

Ur of the Chaldees

Woolley's greatest achievement was his excavation of Ur of the Chaldees. This city near the Gulf was the one left behind by Abraham and his family in search of a new land in which their descendants could become a great nation.

Those biblical critics who had not relegated Abraham to the land of legend, had him down as an illiterate sheikh who deserted a primitive settlement to chase superstitions through the desert.

As Sir Leonard Woolley's findings were released during the 1920s quite a battalion of 'higher critics' were having to find something else to talk about . . . .

What Woolley dug up was a populous city with large buildings — *so* large they presupposed the use of some strong means of leverage like a crane — which had served as a political and cultural centre 4,000 and more years ago.

Ur had the most impressive *ziggurat* or temple tower of the Mesopotamian region. Even after four millennia in ruins it measured seventy feet high. It was constructed with well-baked bricks. Almost every brick had an inscription. From these inscriptions Woolley's team read the history of the whole region.

The name Abraham was identified on contract tablets dating from around 2000 BC. Among the witnesses to such contracts appear names like Jacob, Terah, Sarah, Milcah and Laban.

The city contained other temples.

There was an impressive residential quarter. Typically the houses were two storey, with a street door and a rear door leading to a central patio enclosed by kitchens, store rooms and capacious living rooms. Ur had been served by an efficient underground sanitation system (which put to shame the sanitation arrangements in most towns of present-day Iraq).

Several schools were excavated. Cuneiform tablets were found in them. From these tablets it is clear that the wealthier class in Ur — and, because of the size of his flocks and herds, we must include Abraham in this — had a sophisticated grasp of maths, trigonometry, astronomy and geography.

The date of the Exodus

How we interpret the archaeological finds in Egypt very much depends on whether we date the Exodus in the fifteenth century or the thirteenth century BC.

As has been indicated in our dating of the Pentateuch (chapter 2), we believe the fifteenth century date to be accurate. The reasons are both biblical and archaeological.

1 Kings 6:1 is the vital reference point for biblical chronology: *'In the four hundred and eightieth year after the Israelites had come out of Egypt, in the fourth year of Solomon's reign over Israel, in the month of Ziv, the second month, he began to build the temple of the Lord.'* (NIV.) That Solomon began to build his temple in the year 967 BC is not disputed. Hence the date of the Exodus must have been around 1450 BC. The Pharaoh of the Oppression is taken as Thutmoses III. The Pharaoh of the Exodus is taken as Amenhotep II (1450-1425 BC). The period of the wilderness wandering is taken to be from *circa* 1450 — *circa* 1410 BC. And the period thereafter as the years of Joshua's conquest of Canaan.

Among the difficulties of the thirteenth century Exodus under Pharaoh Ramses II is that it places Joshua two centuries before Moses! And distorts the biblical narrative in all kinds of incredible ways. The 1450 BC date for the Exodus harmonizes with God's prophecy to Abraham that the Israelites would serve for 400 years until his plan was ripe for them to occupy Canaan (Genesis 15:13-16). If the period is understood to extend from Abraham, it also harmonizes with the 430 years mentioned in Exodus 12:40 (see footnote in NIV).

The 'late date' view was widely held in the mid-nineteenth century. By the 1890s the 'early date' view was gaining support. Authorities including Max Muller (1897), James Breasted (1897), H. R. R. Hall and A. H. Gardiner (1913), E. Peet

(1922), C. A. F. Knight (1922), J. W. Jack (1925), J. Garstang (1931), T. H. Robinson (1932), A. S. Yahuda (1933), W. J. Phythian-Adams (1934), E. O. James (1935), W. A. F. Blunt (1936), A. Bradford (1936), S. L. Craiger (1936), and Seigfried Horn (1953 and 1978), among others, believe that biblical data taken together with the discovery of the Israel Stele and the evidence of the Tell el Amarna tablets make the 'late date' view untenable.

However, certain modern Egyptologists who take the *late date* view assert, on the basis of it, that there is no archaeological evidence for the Exodus from Egypt. Hence it has become fashionable to doubt whether the Exodus ever actually occurred. Is there archaeological evidence for the Exodus if one accepts the *early date* view?

There is, we believe, archaeological evidence not only for the *early date* Exodus, but for Joseph's contribution to Egyptian history.

Joseph was sold into Egypt about 1847 BC. The transaction occurred at Dothan where Joseph was thrown into a pit or cistern; a tell identified as Dothan has been excavated with a deep cistern at the foot of the gradient.

The sale of Joseph by the Midianite traders to Potiphar is paralleled by many records of *Kan'amu* (Canaanite) slaves. Names like Potiphar are of genuine Egyptian origin. Ankle-length examples of the *'coat of many colours'* are found in pictures of semitic visitors to Egypt. The *'signet ring'*, the *'vesture of fine linen'*, and the *'gold chain about Joseph's neck'* to which the Bible refers all accord with Egyptian custom.

The biblical record indicates that Joseph predicted to Pharaoh that there would be *'seven years of plenty'* and *'seven years of famine'*, and asserts that he was appointed to the office of *merper* or *vizier* to make appropriate preparations. This incident is likely to have taken place at the beginning of the Twelfth Dynasty; perhaps under Pharaoh Sesostris I. Sesostris was the pharaoh who built the first large obelisk called the Pillar of On. The Bible indicates that Joseph married the daughter of the priest of On.

The important office to which Sesostris appointed Joseph, and the accoutrements of that office, are often mentioned in inscriptions. Doubt was once cast on the possibility of a mere Canaanite slave's promotion to high honours in Egypt. But archaeology has discovered many striking parallels. Neri-Ra, a Canaanite, became armour-bearer to Pharaoh. Ben-Mat-Ana, also a Canaanite, was raised to the important office of interpreter. Yankhamu, a semite, actually became deputy to Pharaoh Amenhotep III with charge over the granaries of the Delta. There are many other examples.

The Bible indicates that Sesostris gave the order that everyone should 'bow the knee' to Joseph. This detail puzzled the experts for some time. Normally the people would not bow to a *vizier*. But archaeology has turned up evidence of such a *vizier* under Sesostris I. The vizier's name, according to the inscription, was Min-tu-ho-tip. In the early Twelfth Dynasty a canal, still known as *Bahr Yusuf* — Joseph's Canal — was dug, possibly as part of his preparation for the famine years.

The Tomb of Amani dates from the reign of Sesostris I. On the wall of this tomb is a record in hieroglyphs of how Amani helped prepare for a coming famine; and how, through good management, Egypt survived the famine well.

An early Eighteenth Dynasty pharaoh, perhaps Thutmoses I, was the 'new king over Egypt, which knew not Joseph' (Exodus 1:8). A spirit of nationalism would appear to have been fostered. This was not the first time there had been such an upsurge, and that foreigners had borne the brunt of the nationalistic spirit. A century earlier — in 1567 BC — the Asiatic *Hyksos* had been expelled from Egypt.

The suspicion and hatred against the semitic Israelites which had begun under Thutmoses I was continued during the short

This black stone pillar 2.5 metres high records the laws of King Hammurabi of Babylon *circa* 1792-1750 BC. This famous law code is often compared with the laws of Moses.

The Black Obelisk records the triumphs of King Shalmaneser III of Assyria. Discovered at Nimrud in 1846 it depicts, among other things, Jehu, king of Israel, 'Son of Omri', bringing tribute to the Assyrians.

reign of his successor, Thutmoses II, the fourth ruler of the Eighteenth Dynasty.

The untimely death of Thutmoses II left his widow Hatshepsut as *de facto* ruler. From 1504 to 1482 BC she ruled with a strong but steady hand. She built a grandiose mortuary-temple at Deir el-Bahri in western Thebes, still considered by many to be the most beautiful of the Egyptian temples.

The character of Hatshepsut gained from the Bible is not unlike that of the historical Hatshepsut. Both chronology and historical circumstances point to her as the foster mother of Moses. Records indicate that she hated Thutmoses III, her nephew, who had been foisted on her as co-ruler (but whom she successfully kept in the background for many years). She may well have intended Moses as her successor. Josephus Flavius connects this princess of the House of Thutmoses with the 'princess' who found Moses 'in the bulrushes' (Exodus 2:5 *et seq*) and proceeded to make arrangements for his upbringing and education.

In naming the baby as she did, she conferred upon him a name common in her family. Since she had found him in the river it may have been in her mind to have named him after the river god, Hapi. It is probable that she called him Hapi-moses, 'Born of the God Hapi'. Later Moses rejected the name of the Egyptian god. Hence his name simply meant 'Born of'.

From the beginning of her reign Hatshepsut announced her intention of reigning as a man. This may be the reason why many representations of her are in male attire. In addition to the many temples and obelisks which survive to this day she erected the Giant Obelisk (100 feet) at Karnak.

Whatever her plans had been for Moses, he mysteriously disappeared from the scene. It is likely that by this time Hatshepsut's strong-minded ways had excited the jealousy of her over-shadowed co-ruler, Thutmoses III. At all events, as soon as she was dead, he began a policy of defacing the monuments she had erected.

The death of Hatshepsut inaugurated the last and worst phase of the oppression of the Israelites. Thutmoses III reigned as sole ruler for thirty-three years (1482-1450 BC). He had the reputation of a merciless tyrant and conducted successful military campaigns in Palestine and Syria. The most important historical monument to Thutmoses III is his famous inscription on a pylon of the Temple at Karnak. Here we find the earliest references to Canaan in the Egyptian royal inscriptions. It describes the conquests of Thutmoses III, and names, familiar from the Bible story, recur, including Kadesh, Megiddo, Dothan, Damascus, Hazor, Carmel, Joppa, Gath and Bethel. Among the place names recorded on this monument are two which have special interest for us: Joseph-El and Jacob-Er. Scholars are uneasy at suggesting that these names have anything to do with the biblical Joseph or Jacob. Nevertheless their occurrence at this point in time is interesting.

The successor of Thutmoses III, Amenhotep II (1450-1425 BC), was probably the pharaoh of the Exodus. His reputation for cruelty equalled that of his predecessor. Uprisings in different parts of the Egyptian empire were put down with utmost ferocity.

Near the pyramid of Sesostris II, a city was excavated by Sir Flinders Petrie in 1891. Rosalie David published a book in 1986 highlighting some of Petrie's discoveries; *among them, that the entire city was occupied by semitic slaves.* Following the 'late date' Exodus theory, Rosalie David does not make the connection between this excavation and the Israelites of the Bible. She does, however, recount one of Petrie's discoveries germane to the biblical record; that underneath the floor of many houses were boxes containing the skeletons of babies a few months old at death. This may or may not be connected with the policy pursued by Pharaoh and described in Exodus

1:11-22. Even more interesting is Rosalie David's assertion that the departure of the semitic slaves was 'sudden and unpremeditated'. That slaves could simply pack up and leave is puzzling unless you accept the Bible accounts.

The Bible indicates that the economy of Egypt was severely disrupted immediately prior to the Exodus. In the Leiden Museum in Holland is the Ipuwer Papyrus. It is dated late Twelfth Dynasty and includes this haunting quotation: 'Plague stalketh through the land and blood is everywhere. Nay, but many dead men are buried in the river. Nay, but the river *is* blood. Does a man drink thereof? He rejects it. . . . Corn has perished everywhere.' Is this a contemporary account of the phenomena described in more detail in Exodus 7:14-10:29?

There is one final pointer to the Exodus. Firstborn sons throughout Egypt died on the eve of the departure of the Israelites (Exodus 11:1-10; 12:29). When the Pharaoh of the Exodus, Amenhotep II, died, he was succeeded, not by his firstborn son, but by a younger son. He took the title Thutmoses IV.

Digging up Israel

The conquest of Canaan

We have accepted 1450 BC as the date of the Exodus. Hence we must accept *circa* 1410-1400 BC as the period of Joshua's conquest of Canaan.

The history of the Egyptian Empire, chiselled in hieroglyphs on its walls and cuneiform on its tablets, points up the accuracy of our dating.

In 1400 BC Pharaoh Amenhotep the Magnificent was still on the throne of Egypt. His wealth and power was beyond the dreams of any previous monarch. His imperial writ still ran to distant Syria and Canaan. At first glance it seems an unpropitious time for Joshua to attack the outposts of the Empire.

However, though the centre of the Empire seemed as firm as ever, the circumference was beginning to show signs of breaking up as Amenhotep's luxury-sodden reign progressed. A letter to Burna-Buriash, King of Babylon, *circa* 1380, speaks of disaffection among the vassal kings of Canaan in the reign of his father (which included the years 1410-1400 BC). The Tell el Amarna Tablets describe a tumultuous situation around the 1400 period. These tablets demonstrate clearly that in the years of Joshua's conquest, Egyptian prestige in Canaan had hit decline. The Pharaoh was engrossed in building artificial lakes, engaging in hunts, and was taking very little interest in the affairs of state. By doing this he had weakened his vassal kings in Canaan. They believed that the Egyptian Pharaoh was pulling back. Hence there was a power vacuum in

Canaan as Joshua's armies crossed the Jordan. This power vacuum the Israelites were about to fill.

THE TELL EL AMARNA TABLETS

Tell el Amarna is situated on the Upper Nile. In 1887 someone living there began poking about in a rubbish heap. There they uncovered a collection of inscribed clay tablets. In the early months after the discovery hundreds of these tablets were destroyed by ignorant, over-eager 'excavators'.

The scholars arrived in time to rescue 300 of them.

After considerable study these tablets turned out to be the buried records of the once-royal capital of *Akhnaton*. The tablets were, in effect, letters and despatches sent out during the years 1380 to 1360 BC to the Egyptian court.

Most of the tablets had been written by kings of Canaanite cities named in the Bible — including the king of Jerusalem — and written *to* the pharaohs.

All the letters were written in Babylonian cuneiform. Since both the Canaanites and the Egyptians had a well-developed language and alphabet of their own, it would appear that they were using this form of cuneiform as the language of diplomacy.

The letters reveal that Canaan, a province of the Egyptian Empire, was in a state of extreme turmoil.

The vassal kings were sending frenzied appeals to the pharaohs. They needed help! Formidable invaders were attacking from the north and east! If reinforcements did not arrive soon the country would be lost for ever! Fortress city after fortress city was falling into the enemy's hands. . . .

The invaders from the north were the restless Hittites. The Tell el Amarna Tablets tell the story of the Hittite invasion of northern Palestine in the early fourteenth century. Hittite inscriptions lend another dimension to the happenings of those years. At the same time as the Canaanite kings were making frantic pleas for help to their Egyptian overlord they were in treacherous communication with the Hittite invaders. In the years of Joshua's invasion Canaan had reached a pretty pass.

However, the Tell el Amarna Tablets also make clear that the dreaded Hittite invasion of the heart of Canaan never materialized. Happenings elsewhere in their northern empire diverted Hittite attention, and their forces withdrew — leaving Canaan wide open to the Israelite forces attacking from the East.

Among the Tell el Amarna Tablets are the letters of Arad-Hiba, King of Jerusalem, complaining to Pharaoh of the depredations of a people called the *Habiru*. Elsewhere in the *Tell el Amarna* record we read: 'The Habiru are now capturing the fortresses of the Pharaoh. Not a single governor remains among them to my lord the King: all have perished. . . . The land of the King is lost to the Habirus. And now indeed the city of the territory of Jerusalem, *Bet-Ninib*, has been captured. . . .'

The identification of the *Habiru* and the Hebrews is a rather obvious one. More especially since the circumstances of the *Habiru* invasion from the east are precisely those of the Hebrew invasion, as regards date, location, results and the actual place names concerned.

The Tell el Amarna Tablets are painting from the Canaanite side the same picture which the historian of the biblical books of Joshua and Judges paints from the Hebrew side.

The Tell el Amarna Tablets present one difficulty, however. It is next to impossible to identify cuneiform names from their context. Hence it is disappointing, at first sight, that no biblical personal names are identified with certainty. It is also beyond question that the tablets date from the period immediately *after* Joshua's initial incursion into Canaan. Hence they are largely concerned with the battles fought and won by his successors.

The fall of Jericho

The first Canaanite city to fall to Joshua's armies was Jericho. The Bible accounts describe how Jericho's walls fell and how, thereafter, the city was gutted by fire.

Jericho represents one of the most impressive tells in Palestine. Archaeologists believe that it is the oldest city on earth. Indeed, that its greatest days were over long before the Israelite armies surrounded it.

During the age of scientific archaeology the tell Jericho has been subjected to two intensive excavations.

The first of these was undertaken by Professor John Garstang and his team from the University of Liverpool between 1930 and 1936. Garstang grabbed the headlines and shook the critics when he published his finds. In many parts of the tell he found the stumps of walls, clear evidence that the major part of the walls had 'fallen down'. While the critics sniggered, Garstang and his team persisted. There were two walls, parallel, with a space of 15 feet between them. Buildings had rested across the tops of these walls. A violent conflagration had overtaken the city, completely destroying it. Garstang dated this conflagration to 1400 BC, a date he reached on the evidence of Egyptian scarabs from tombs he opened around Jericho. This accorded with the 'early date' for the Exodus and the Conquest. Hence Garstang's findings were accepted by the most scholarly archaeologists.

The second excavation of Jericho was headed by Dr. Kathleen Kenyon of the University of London and took place between 1952 and 1958. With others she had believed that there was something 'too good to be true' about Garstang's findings. She applied her trench system to Jericho and, after some years of research, began to publish her findings.[1]

Immediately those in the popular press who scented a 'good story' polarized the findings of Garstang and the findings of Kenyon. Kenyon, it was reported, dated the truncated walls to a period long before the Israelite conquest and asserted that erosion by the elements made it impossible to find any traces of Joshua's Jericho.

Certainly Dame Kathleen was more sceptical about the evidence than Garstang had been. Nevertheless, in her book *Archaeology in the Holy Land*,[2] she conceded that Jericho had been destroyed by fire, that there was widespread evidence of the fire-scorched stumps of walls to which Garstang had referred, and that the destruction had covered an area about 56 feet by 24 feet. In addition she found evidence of a partial rebuilding programme in Jericho undertaken in the historical period which — if we accept the 'early date' Conquest — would have followed Joshua's destruction. Despite that, in the most recent revision of her book *The Bible and Recent Archaeology*,[3] it is made crystal clear that Dr. Kenyon did not associate what she found with the biblical narrative.

Dame Kathleen found evidence of widespread destruction in different parts of Palestine dating from the same period. This destruction affected cities as far apart as the metropolis of Hazor, north of Galilee, and Lachish, south of Jerusalem. Kenyon attributed this destruction to the Asiatic *Hyksos* and two Egyptian attempts to re-assert control in Canaan. According to the biblical narrative the cities, including Hazor and Lachish, at this time blackened by destruction, were taken by Joshua's forces. It is, therefore, possible that the damage she attributes to the *Hyksos* and the Egyptians was in fact inflicted by the Israelites.

In 1990 American archaeologist Professor Bryant Wood reported new and important information about the destruction of Jericho. He had been studying the excavation reports of Kenyon that were published after her death. He found that she had misdated pottery from the last major city of Jericho. She had dated it 1550 BC, having looked for foreign, painted pottery and found it to be absent. She failed to recognize the now better-known local pottery which existed in profusion in the final destruction level of the tell. In addition Professor Wood actually found some of the very painted pottery in Garstang's pottery bags in the Louvre that Kenyon had missed. Wood's findings were published in the *Biblical Archaeology Reviews* for 1990. Hence the findings at Jericho fit the biblical account even better than anyone previously recognized. Everything points to 1400 BC as the date of Jericho's destruction.

Professor Garstang believed that, down to 1360 BC, there was considerable archaeological evidence to corroborate the settlement of Canaan by the Israelites. But from that date until the coming of the Philistines, 200 years later, we are very much in the dark. The Bible itself provides very little detail.

Tablets discovered at Beth-shan in 1923 provide evidence of a Hittite attack on Hazor — a city which Joshua had acknowledged as the strategic key to the control of the northlands — *and* contain the first Egyptian attempt to reproduce the name *Habiru* or Hebrew.

Garstang suggests that Judges 3:30 — *'The land had rest, fourscore years'* — applies to the period of the Pharaoh Rameses the Great and his successors, during which Canaan, along with other adjacent lands, was overawed by the near presence of the powerful Egyptian policemen.

But Garstang and Kenyon are agreed that this period of 'rest' was the calm before the storm. 'About the year 1200 BC there was a catastrophic interruption in the civilization of the whole of the Eastern Mediterranean,' writes Kenyon, 'producing a Dark Age very like that following the Roman Empire in Europe 1,600 years later, and was brought about by similar events, the incursions of barbarian groups.'[4]

THE ISRAEL STELE

The Israel *Stele* was discovered by Sir Flinders Petrie in 1896. Conveniently it is self-dated in 'the third year of Merenptah' (1223 BC).

The Israel *Stele* contains a great deal of valuable information which corroborates the biblical narrative. In addition it is the first 'document' outside the Bible on which the actual name *Israel* appears.

The obvious conclusion from this is that by the thirteenth century the Israelites were well settled in Canaan and were known by foreign powers to be its rulers.

Before the Israel *Stele* was discovered, the view that the Israelites remained in Egypt until *circa* 1220 BC — the 'late date' view — had remained almost unchallenged. Thus Rameses was described as 'the Pharaoh of the Oppression' and Merenptah as 'the Pharaoh of the Exodus'.

Taken together, the Tell el Amarna Tablets and the Israel *Stele* provide convincing evidence that the Hebrews had left Egypt and settled in Canaan long before the days of Pharaoh Rameses. However, some 'late date' scholars still refuse to abandon their view arguing that the *Habiru* (mentioned in the Tell el Amarna Tablets) were not in fact the Hebrews. Some argue, indeed, that what the inscriptions actually prove was that the Hebrews had never left Canaan in the first place. . . .

The Philistines

The barbarians came from the sea and very nearly wrested the Promised Land from the Israelites. The Philistines are believed to have come from the Aegean islands by way of Crete. They attacked Egypt, Palestine, and the Hittite country. Though they failed to force their way into Egypt, they successfully settled the maritime plain of Palestine.

Evidence of Philistine destruction has been excavated at Askelon, Ashdod and Ekron. At Tezer a Philistine house of the type which Samson pulled down on the heads of his enemies (Judges 16:29) has been excavated.

The united kingdom of Israel

The period of the united kingdom of Israel lasted for under a century. The kings were Saul, David and Solomon. In retrospect these were looked upon as the glory days of Israel's history. However, there is only meagre archaeological evidence for this brief span of time.

Excavation of Old Jerusalem commenced under the Palestine Exploration Fund in 1865. The original city of Jerusalem was on the Hill Ophel, a spur running south of Temple Mount. Dr. Kenyon asserted, however, that part of Israelite Jerusalem was under the present-day Old City. She predicted that, as people excavated beneath their homes, they would dig up the ancient past. This has proved to be true, especially under the Jewish quarter, in recent years.

But most concerted excavation has centred on the Hill Ophel, flanked by steep slopes with the Kidron Valley to the east and the Tyropoeon Valley to the west. These steep valleys, together with the proximity of a water source — the Gihon Spring — account for the original settlement.

The Palestine Exploration Fund excavators found traces of an original occupation dating back as far as 3000 BC. As a walled city Ophel seems to have been fortified just prior to 2000 BC, and there are signs of mingled Amorite and Hittite constructions of considerable strength. This gives point to Ezekiel's remark; *'Your mother was an Hittite, and your father an Amorite.'* Ezekiel 16:45.

Between 1923 and 1925 a portion of wall on the eastern crest of Ophel was excavated. Prior to David's conquest the name of the city had been *Jebus.* The Jebusite walls, and signs of the breach made by David's well-known assault upon the place, can still be seen. More interesting still, a combination of tunnels, including a vertical shaft, was discovered. This had given the Jebusites their access to water. The vertical shaft had been that up which Joab and his men had crawled to take the defenders in the rear, and for David to take a town the Jebusites had believed impregnable (1 Chronicles 11:6). The shaft has usually been known by the name of its discoverer, Warren's Shaft.

During the 1960s further excavations were launched by the British School of Archaeology. More walls were discovered, some dating from the Jebusite period, others from the davidic period. Some made a distinction between the rough and hasty masonry associated with David, and the more carefully dressed stones of Solomon's period. In the later Jebusite period and during David's reign a series of terraces had been constructed as the basis for a more grandiose town. Solomon and his successors had enlarged on these terraces and extended them, building staircases from the most northerly point of the Hill Ophel to Temple Mount.

It was on Temple Mount — the Mount Moriah of earlier biblical history — that Solomon built his palace and his vast temple to the Lord. The fact that, in a later age, Herod the Great covered the whole area with a vast platform, and that this vast platform is now occupied by Muslim shrines, has prevented meaningful excavation, though a few rooms, stables and cisterns have been discovered beneath the present-day paved area. Of the palace and the temple there are no certain traces.

David pursued an expansionist foreign policy. His former 'oppressors' were themselves oppressed: Moab, Ammon and Edom. All were subjugated. More surprisingly the Arameans were defeated and Damascus was annexed. Under David and Solomon the Israelites controlled by far the larger part of the territory from the Euphrates to the borders of Egypt, though the Philistine towns remained fiercely independent. David welded together the peoples from simple hill villages, formerly united only by religious ties, into an organized kingdom. Of this kingdom Jerusalem was both the religious and political focus.

The divided kingdoms

With the death of Solomon — *circa* 970 BC — came the division of the kingdoms. The northern tribes rebelled against the luxuries and excesses of Solomon's Jerusalem and then, ironically, patterned their Northern Kingdom of Israel on Solomon's reign. In the Southern Kingdom of Judah, including Jerusalem, where the luxurious excesses had taken place, there was a reaction. The Southern Kingdom of Judah went back to the simplicity of an earlier period.

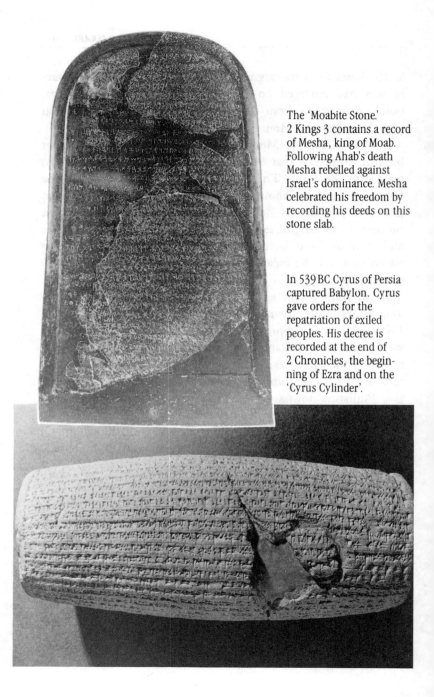

The 'Moabite Stone.' 2 Kings 3 contains a record of Mesha, king of Moab. Following Ahab's death Mesha rebelled against Israel's dominance. Mesha celebrated his freedom by recording his deeds on this stone slab.

In 539 BC Cyrus of Persia captured Babylon. Cyrus gave orders for the repatriation of exiled peoples. His decree is recorded at the end of 2 Chronicles, the beginning of Ezra and on the 'Cyrus Cylinder'.

Solomon had fortified the northern city of Megiddo (1 Kings 9:15). Here shades of his magnificence can be seen in the Tell Megiddo. To uncover signs of magnificence in the period after Solomon's death we must look exclusively north of the frontier between Judah and Israel.

The earlier kings of the North had no fixed abode. Their first base was *Shechem* (Nablus). Then their capital was transferred to *Tirzah* (at the time of Baasha, the third king). About 885 BC Omri laid siege to Tirzah, captured it and the usurper Zimri, and made plans to build a new capital elsewhere. Excavations by the Ecole Biblique have identified the Tell el Far'ah as Tirzah. The evidence of Omri's violent destruction is there in abundance; the contents of the houses are buried in the debris of their super-structures.

From this period on, the important archaeological evidence changes. At long last we find contemporary inscriptions which deal explicitly with Hebrew history. We recognize familiar Bible names and situations in independent records written by men who were actually contemporaries of Elijah, Amos and Isaiah. The inscriptions, however, whether on stone or clay, were prepared by potentates with one eye on posterity and the other on immediate self-glorification. But, for all that, they are most illuminating.

Omri, King of Israel, 886-874 BC, is the first Hebrew king whose name appears in the monuments of antiquity. His name was chiselled on the Stone of Mesha and upon the cuneiform records of Assyria. This is an indication that the world was waking up to the importance of the Hebrews. Omri's reign is very lightly passed over in the Bible (1 Kings 16:23-28), but the independent records provide ample evidence that the impression that he made on his contemporaries was by no means small. Indeed, the lands of northern Palestine were known as 'The Land of Omri' to the Assyrians.

King Omri transferred the capital of Israel from *Tirzah* to

Samaria (1 Kings 16:24). Kathleen Kenyon says that, on the evidence of pottery, 'where Tell el Far'ah stops, Samaria begins'. She found evidence that Omri moved, not only his court but, in all probability, all of the inhabitants, complete with all of their property.

The credit for the excavation of Samaria belongs first to a Harvard expedition under Reisner in 1909 and, second, to a British expedition under Crofoot in the 1930s. Omri had grand ideas for Samaria. The excavated buildings and layout of the capital demonstrate this eloquently. The city had a good strategic situation, lying athwart the main north-south route, hence in easy contact with Phoenicia and in a position to spot and prevent any aggressive advances from Judah. It was to facilitate trade that Omri married his son Ahab to Jezebel of Tyre.

'Excavation confirms the biblical account that Omri founded his town on a virgin site,' says Kenyon, who worked as an assistant to Crofoot. Samaria was laid out as a new city dominated by a royal quarter. In this it resembled Solomon's Jerusalem. The royal quarter was built on a 'summit plateau' above the level of the remainder of the city. The building of the city was extended and completed by Ahab who succeeded his father within six years of the move to the new capital.

The Assyrian menace loomed large during the reigns of both Omri and Ahab. The cuneiform record describing the Assyrian victory at the Battle of Karkar on the Shalmanezer's Monolith Inscription, includes an important reference to Ahab, King of Israel, son of Omri. 1 Kings 22:39 refers to *the ivory house* built by Ahab. Excavations indicate that Ahab enlarged the palace built by his father and added a tremendously heavy double wall completely encircling it, plus a massive royal treasury with an elaborate system of store chambers. Ivory wall plaques were excavated in Ahab's palace at Samaria in 1933.

The same ivory had already been discovered in Sargon's palace at Nimrud taken there after the fall of Samaria at the hands of the Assyrians. The prophet Amos (6:4) had fulminated powerfully against the people of Samaria who *'lie upon beds of ivory, and stretch themselves upon their couches'*. A bed of ivory, with solid ivory legs and beautiful carving, which doubtless originated in Samaria, has actually been found at *Arslan-Tash* in northern Syria.

The Omri-Ahab palace was Phoenician in style. Along with Jezebel, Ahab may also have imported Phoenician craftsmen. Ahab's census provided evidence that 7,000 of *'all the children of Israel'* inhabited the city of Samaria. There may have been many more foreigners as well. One hundred and fifty years later Sargon deported 27,290 people from the city.

The Moabite Stone, discovered in 1868, contains a royal inscription written in Hebrew. About three-and-a-half feet in height, two feet wide and two feet thick, the Moabite Stone with its inscription is of immense importance. It describes the historical situation; Omri had triumphed over Moab for *'many days'* before his death, and Ahab had inherited the tribute payable by Moab (2 Kings 3:4).

The supremacy of Israel lasted half way through the reign of Ahab. On Ahab's death the Moabite rebellion came to a head and his son Jehoram marched from Samaria to suppress it (2 Kings 3:5). At first Israel, in alliance with Jehoshaphat of Judah, won a victory at the Battle of the Blood Red Water (2 Kings 3:22), but eventually Mesha sacrificed his eldest son upon the wall and defeated the Hebrew alliance, so that they *'departed from him, and returned to their own land'* (2 Kings 3:27). It is to this last Moabite victory that the stone refers in greatest length.

Cut off from worship at the temple in Jerusalem, the northern kings set up religious centres at the northern and southern extremities of their kingdom: Dan and Bethel. Excavations at the Tell Dan have shown that the same style of architecture was used as at Samaria. A rectangular summit (or high place) has been excavated, approached by a flight of steps. Many of the large public buildings at Megiddo belong to Ahab's reign. Among them was a southern palace. To Ahab's reign also belongs the huge water shaft at Megiddo; a major undertaking, providing direct access to the spring from the interior of the town. It consists of a vertical shaft 35 metres deep, plus a horizontal tunnel 63 metres long. The even more impressive water system at Hazor also belongs to Ahab's reign. In Hazor, as in Megiddo and Samaria, a royal-administrative quarter was built during Ahab's reign, separate from the residential quarters.

With Ahab employed in ambitious building projects, the Assyrian advance continued inexorably into the Northern Kingdom. This was the period of Elisha's ruthless suppression of the cult of Baal, of Amos and Hosea hurling spoken and written thunderbolts against the godless luxury of Israel. This is a period rich in documentation. Among the primary sources are Uckenbill's *Ancient Records of Assyria*, Shalmanezer's Statue Inscription from Assur, and the Black Obelisk of Shalmanezer III. The Black Obelisk depicts Jehu, King of Israel, doing homage, and is dated from 841 BC. These sources not only corroborate the biblical narrative, but they provide additional details to it.

After the accession of Tiglath-Pileser III in Ninevah the advance of Assyria was unstoppable. Any number of inscriptions bear out the record of the biblical books of Kings and Chronicles, as do the archaeological excavations of Dame Kathleen Kenyon. The end of Stratum IV at Megiddo represents the destruction brought about by the Assyrian attack *circa* 734 BC. The violent destruction of Stratum V at Hazor is to be ascribed to the same cause. Dame Kathleen: 'On most sites there is, in fact, evidence of violent events during this period.'

The northern part of the Northern Kingdom was annexed first by Tiglath-Pileser III. Many Israelites were carried into captivity. Ten years later, in 724 BC, Shalameser V besieged Samaria. It resisted for two years. Then fell to his successor Sargon II in 722 BC. Sargon went on south to defeat the Egyptians. On his way back in 720 BC he carried the rest of the tribes of Israel into captivity.

The Fall of the Southern Kingdom

The fall of the Northern Kingdom made a deep impression in Jerusalem. This is indicated by the reforms of Hezekiah and the increased influence of the prophetic schools in diplomatic affairs. For a time Isaiah completely controlled the policy of his king. He saw clearly that the real issue was between Assyria and Egypt, and that Judah's only hope of avoiding destruction lay in neutrality. The description of Isaiah (20:1) of Sargon's expedition against Ashdod is borne out and amplified in the Khorsabad Inscription and also in the Cylinder of Sargon discovered in Ashurbanipal's library at Ninevah.

In 705 BC Sennacherib began to ravage Judah. Lachish was captured and sacked; the Bible describes it, archaeology authenticates it. Jerusalem was besieged but held out. Hezekiah bought off the Assyrians by paying tribute. Judah had bought time for another century but was, in effect, a semi-independent vassal. Dr. Kenyon writes, 'On a number of sites archaeological evidence has been found of these events, for their effect was so cataclysmic that there is seldom much doubt in the correlation of the archaeological and historical (biblical) evidence.'[5]

Though Jerusalem did not fall to the Assyrians it was placed in desperate straits. Hezekiah and his masons became active. The town walls were repaired. Most importantly Hezekiah and his engineers carried out a massive work of civil engineering.

Hitherto the city had been dependent upon the Gihon Spring outside the walls and upon the rock-cisterns for rainwater. But now Hezekiah *'made a pool, and a conduit, and brought water into the city'* (2 Kings 20:20). Hezekiah's engineers built a tunnel through 1,800 feet of living rock from the Gihon Spring (outside the city wall) to the Pool of Siloam (well inside the city). This was of vital importance in withstanding a siege, more especially since Warren's Shaft had long been filled with rubble, forgotten and abandoned. The achievement is referred to several times in 2 Kings and 2 Chronicles.

Hezekiah's Tunnel has been known for a long period, but, in 1880, Dr. Conrad Schick — who excavated the Garden Tomb — discovered the Siloam Inscription when wading through the conduit under the walls of Old Jerusalem. The tunnel had been built by two separate groups of workmen chiselling from either end. The inscription records the excitement of the two parties of workmen as they met under the heart of the Hill Ophel. In the excavations of 1909-1911 the whole tunnel was cleared out.

In 621 BC the Assyrian Empire gave way to the Babylonian Empire. Babylon conquered Assyrian territories. In campaigns in 598 and 589-587 Nebuchadnezzar finally annexed Judah. 'Archaeology fully supports the biblical evidence of the disastrous effect of the Babylonian campaign which brought this period to a close. Large numbers of towns were destroyed and never occupied again. Of these, Tell Beit Mirsim and Beth-Shemesh are typical examples.' Beersheba was another. The precise dating of the fall of these cities to the Babylonian armies can be pinpointed by pottery. [6]

Zedekiah's revolt against Nebuchadnezzar led to the final destruction of Jerusalem in 586 BC (2 Kings 24:17-25). Nebuchadnezzar had inscriptions chiselled which are still extant and bear out the biblical records. The Jerusalem excavations undertaken between 1961 and 1967 uncovered evidence among the collapsed terraces, retaining walls and houses of the violence of the destruction.

Return from exile

In 540 BC the Babylonian Empire was annexed by the Persians under Cyrus. The Persian Empire pursued a policy of toleration toward national cultures and religions. Evidence for this policy has been found on the Cylinder of Cyrus found by Hormuz Rassan in Babylon, dating from 536 BC.

Successive leaders led parties back to Jerusalem. In 520 BC Zerubbabel rebuilt the temple, way down-market of the grand edifice of Solomon.

In 444 BC Nehemiah and his masons restored the walls of the city. However, the homogeneity of the Jewish people had been disrupted to an extent that it was irreparable.

No new kingdom could grow up around the partially rebuilt Jerusalem. Many Jews, in fact, remained behind in Babylonia and Persia.

Those who returned were continually at loggerheads with what Nehemiah calls 'the peoples of the land'. The returned exiles despised these people as being of mixed blood. This was the beginning of the Samaritan schism. The occasion of this was when Manasseh, grandson of High Priest Eliashib, was driven out by Nehemiah on the grounds of intermarriage. Sanballat, governor of Samaria, built a temple on Mount Gerazim, a rival to the temple at Jerusalem.

Despite painstaking excavation between 1961 and 1967 little remains of Zerubbabel's second temple, except for the southeast corner of the temple platform. Nehemiah's walls, however, have proved more durable. A wall on the crest of Ophel, previously ascribed to an earlier period, was found to date from the period of Nehemiah's rebuilding.

The chief reason why so little of Zerubbabel's temple has

206

survived: Herod the Great extended its area into a large platform and built a far grander edifice over it.

References
[1] Kathleen Kenyon, *Archaeology in the Holy Land*, fourth edition (1979), pages vii-ix, 5, 14, 328, 331-332.
[2] Ibid, pages 181 *et seq*.
[3] Kathleen Kenyon, *The Bible and Recent Archaeology* (revised and partially rewritten by P. R. S. Moody in 1987), page 73. It should be noted that this substantially revised edition of Dame Kathleen's earlier work made its appearance almost a decade after her death.
[4] Kathleen Kenyon, *Archaeology in the Holy Land*, fourth edition (1979), page 212.
[5] Ibid, page 288.
[6] Ibid, pages 296, 299.

Herod: the great builder

'Jesus was born in Bethlehem of Judaea in the days of Herod the king.' Matthew 2:1.

And this 'Herod the king', whose paranoid dynasty, from their cameo parts, provides a chill of menace to the Gospel story, Who was he? And how did he come to stand so near centre-stage at the crossroads of time? And what did he do to merit the epithet 'Great'?

The desert kingdom

Herod was born in Idumaea (Edom) south of the Dead Sea, son of a self-made king (insofar as *any* king could be self made and still perch on the desert edge of the Roman empire). Before the coming of the Romans (Jewish) King John Hyrcanus had conquered Idumaea and allowed its inhabitants to live on condition that they converted to Judaism. In 63 BC Palestine — and Idumaea — fell to Pompey and, soon, Roman rule was followed by Roman roads, Roman aqueducts and Roman (hellenistic) architecture.

Roman peace was slower in coming.

Nabataea, which bordered Idumaea to the east, rebelled. Idumaean chief Antipater found a way of discrediting his own king, persuading the Nabataeans to pay tribute and ingratiating himself with the Romans.

The Romans had sent Mark Antony to quell the uprising. Antipater supplied his army and, by gaining the confidence of the rebels, prepared the way for the Romans to destroy them.

Antipater made sure he was in at the kill. The rebellion

crushed, he was now *de facto* ruler of the region. By switching support from Pompey to Julius Caesar in the nick of time as they struggled for supremacy, Antipater was preparing himself for kingship. As he marched into Egypt with Julius Caesar he thought he was king already. On his return he was made a Roman citizen and procurator of Judaea.

Among Antipater's first acts as procurator was to make his son, Phasael, prefect of Jerusalem — and his son Herod governor of Galilee.

Herod's rise

Young Herod had taken full advantage of Mark Antony's presence in the desert kingdom. The two had become firm friends. Caesar ensured that Herod received an education in Rome.

Herod's father had never ascended the throne. Herod was determined that *he* would. Under his veneer of Hellenistic culture this Eastern-despot-in-the-making would stop at nothing to achieve his objective.

Herod's enemies were of the Hyrcanus family who still dominated the Sanhedrin in Jerusalem. Overriding their authority he pulled off a brilliant coup by — in a series of lightning strikes — crushing banditry in Galilee. The family Hyrcanus objected but the Roman Proconsul of Syria backed the victor — and appointed Herod governor of *Coele-Syria*.

Herod moved closer to a crown by marrying the beautiful Mariamne, granddaughter of Hyrcanus, one time king of Idumaea.

But in those fraught days of intrigue and political murder, Herod still had to do some fancy footwork.

Judaea was under threat from the Persians in the east and a pro-Persian party on the home front. In 44 BC Caesar was assassinated and Antipater poisoned. Roman interests in Palestine again looked vulnerable. Mark Antony returned at the head of a legion. Antigonus, king of Idumaea 40-37 BC, backed Persia. Herod appealed to Rome. Rome appointed him king.

But his throne was perilously insecure. For one thing the sanhedrin was still controlled by his enemies. And then there was his friendship with Mark Antony. . . .

Herod's ties with Mark Antony were close.

In 31 BC, at the Battle of Actium, the fleet of Mark Antony and Cleopatra of Egypt was defeated by Octavian. Antony and Cleopatra committed suicide. Octavian became Augustus Caesar, master of the world.

For Herod, friend of defeated Antony, the future looked bleak.

But, still in the glad, confident morning of youth and new to the glory of kingship, Herod was not short on audacity.

He sailed for Rome.

Sought an audience with Augustus.

Boldly approached him as one king greeting another.

Instead of minimizing his ties with Antony, he made much of his loyalty to him — and offered the same loyalty to Augustus.

After a triumphal progress in company with Augustus, Herod returned to Palestine, king of the Jews, without a rival.

Herod the builder

'Herod was one of the most passionate builders of antiquity.'[1]

It is in his role as the great builder that Herod, first, appears at his best; second, left to posterity something of such lasting value that his contribution was without equal in his region and in his time.

The hallmark of Herodian masonry were the huge, oblong blocks of stone with smooth margins cut around a central, raised boss.

By the second decade of Herod's reign he had expanded his kingdom to northern Palestine and beyond the Jordan. He had secured his borders, subdued (temporarily) internal resistance, increased his revenues and was, therefore, set to undertake a massive building programme.

The elder Pliny wrote that Herod made Jerusalem 'the most famous of the great cities of the East'. Josephus Flavius in his *Antiquities of the Jews* called Herod's temple a 'work of the greatest piety and excellence that could possibly have been undertaken'.

The temple

But it is unlikely the piety was on Herod's mind when, in 19 BC, he decided on the gargantuan task of rebuilding the Jerusalem temple.

He was still in search of legitimacy. He was not a Jew and was regarded by Jewish leaders with a sneer. Even disdainful, disaffected rabbis and scribes, Sadducees and Pharisees who rejected him as a mountebank — no descendant of David, not even a Jew — might come round if *his* temple outshone Solomon's.

But how to build the grandiose structure of his imagination without interrupting the temple services? How to get around the fact that ordinary workmen could not enter the inner courts of the temple?

His way of surmounting the first difficulty says much for his ingenuity. His ten thousand workmen were instructed not to touch the old building. As regards the most sacred part of the temple, as much as possible was to be prepared off the site before the one thousand wagons were used to haul it into position.

As for the second problem, a thousand priests were trained as stonemasons and carpenters.

The central building followed Solomon's pattern: a porch,

a central hall and the Holy of Holies. The measurements: 164 feet long, with the porch the same in width and height. The structure was of white stone blocks embellished with gold. On the roof golden spikes were erected to prevent the birds from perching or nesting.

This structure was in place in eighteen months. Begun in 20 BC it was completed in 18 BC.

But this was only the beginning of the grand design.

Herod wanted a huge courtyard in which pilgrims could gather. This would be the focus of worship for the whole nation as Solomon's temple had been before the exile. There would be courtyards hemmed in by ante-rooms, colonnades and cloisters.

To make this lavish plan effective it was necessary to build a huge platform over the original Temple Mount with retaining walls around it. The size of the paved area on which Zerubbabel's — and probably Solomon's — Temple had been built was doubled.

To the west the platform extended into the Tyropoeon (Cheesemakers') Valley. The retaining wall, excavated by Sir Charles Warren (in 1867-70) was sunk into bedrock. A large portion of this is still to be seen; it is the Western or Wailing Wall. Some of the Herodian blocks are $16\frac{1}{2}$ feet long by 13 feet wide.

On the other side of the Tyropoeon Valley was the Western Hill on which many lavish homes were built. Edward Robinson (in 1848-52) found the remains of two arches. He believed they were what was left of a great viaduct linking Temple Mount with Western Hill and, therefore, spanning the valley. Since 1968 Benjamin Mazar's excavations have suggested that the arches were part of a grand stairway down into the valley. Certainly there is evidence that there was such a stairway. But Josephus Flavius (*Jewish Wars*, XV ix 3) refers to a magnificent royal platform built by Herod on the Western

Hill and a viaduct spanning the valley to link it to the temple. Wilson's Arch has also been found to have been one of a series of archways supporting a road from the temple platform to the Western Hill.[2]

To the east the retaining walls rose 450 feet from the Kidron Valley. Dame Kathleen Kenyon pointed out that from the south-east corner of Jerusalem's walls Herodian masonry is visible for a distance of 180 metres. Herod's platform 'completely encased' those of Solomon and Zerubbabel. Scarcely a trace of Zerubbabel's temple survives.[3]

The Antonia Fortress

Having paid his dues to God, Herod proceeded to pay his dues to Caesar.

To the north of the beautiful temple compound a huge, ugly, functional fort was built. Its size was such that it dominated the temple. He named it the Antonia Fortress after Mark Antony.

Beneath the Convent of the Sisters of Zion excavators working between 1903 and 1904 found a Roman courtyard. The Lithostratos was, until recently, believed to have been the 'Gabbatha' of John 19:13, the courtyard of the Praetorium. As late as 1982 one authority was prepared to go still further; 'the pavement . . . formed Pilate's Hall of Judgement from which Jesus was led to the cross.'[4] Recent archaeological excavations undertaken by the Hebrew University have cast doubt on the connection between the Lithostratos and the Praetorium.

While conceding that it was of first century origin and, as evidenced by the games etched into its surface, the haunt of soldiers, the Hebrew archaeologists view the Lithostratos as 'the pavement of a forum (a central plaza)'.[5] But British and American scholars remain unconvinced, pointing out the proximity of the 'pavement' to the two great water cisterns (completely excavated and unquestionably a part of Herod's fort).

Herod's Jerusalem palace

By the time the Roman procurators — based at Caesarea for most of the year — had begun to use the Antonia fortress as their headquarters for the thrice-yearly Jewish feasts, Herod built himself another palace. Here too fine examples of Herodian masonry are still to be found.

The palace was located inside the present Jaffa Gate, formerly part of the west wall of the Old City and fronting the Valley of Hinnom. The modern visitor is introduced to it as 'the Citadel' or 'the Tower of David'.

Without question it had no connection with David.

Herod had it built to the south of three highly ornate (and very different) towers. One he named after his wife Mariamne, another after his brother Phasael, the third after his friend Hippicus.

A part of the Phasael tower remains. The original tower has been preserved to the height of sixty-five feet; built with large blocks of stone in standard Herodian style.[6]

Almost certainly it was to this palace that Jesus was brought for his Good Friday trial before Herod's son, Antipas. Luke 23:7-12.

Caesarea

The city of Caesarea on the coast was another of Herod the Great's achievements. It had been established in the Northern Sharon as a Phoenician port in the third century BC.

Between 25 and 13 BC Herod superintended the construction of a new city and a modern harbour. He was determined to make use of the very latest concepts in civil engineering. A number of piers were constructed for the berthing of ships, together with storage buildings and hostels for seamen. Here, as elsewhere, Herod left evidence of his cynical attitude towards religion; under his instruction a number of temples to Augustus were constructed. The entrance to the harbour was flanked by huge statues. The city was well planned with markets, public baths and a theatre which has been excavated, rebuilt and is in use today. Behind its stage the Mediterranean Sea laps the shoreline.

There is much to be seen at Caesarea, but it is scattered along a mile and a half of shoreline. Some of the huge blocks of limestone, 50 feet by 10 feet in size, remain from the great wall constructed to keep out the sea from the harbour. Today most impressive of all is the aqueduct, completely excavated. Once its function was to provide Caesarea with its water source.

After the death of Herod the Great, Caesarea became the headquarters of Roman governors and remained so from AD 6-66. Here it was that the apostle Paul met Felix, Festus and Agrippa. Acts 23:23 — 26:32.

One of the most fascinating discoveries made during the renovation of the amphitheatre is a stone inscription bearing the name of Pontius Pilate.

Palace at Jericho

Two miles west of Old Jericho, where the *Wadi Qelt* opens into the Jordan Valley, Herod built his winter palace. It was first excavated in 1949 and is best viewed from the old, original road from Jerusalem to Jericho as it snakes downward through the lunar landscape towards the Jordan Valley.

Only after excavations begun in 1973 did it become clear that it was, in fact, a winter palace built in characteristic Herodian style and occupied by Herod and his successors.

The palace is built near a good water source; a series of springs come from the wall of the Judean wilderness that fronts the Jordan Valley. The palace site covers three acres. The original building was 57 yards by 52 yards. Late in his reign Herod substantially enlarged his palace at Jericho. He completed a complex of sunken gardens, a vast swimming pool, various halls, and monumental staircases.

In winter Jerusalem temperatures may dip to near freezing, and they are often between 5 and 10 degrees Celsius. In the Jordan Rift Valley, only twenty-five miles away, the temperatures would be at least ten degrees higher.

Other fortress-palaces

As Herod's reign progressed what had once passed for political acumen came to be seen as animal cunning and a paranoid ruthlessness. He was suspicious of everyone, including those nearest to him. Fearing that they were plotting against him he murdered a number of his sons. His propensity to believe the worst led him to execute his favourite wife, Mariamne. In his last years he was an alienated, maddened tyrant wandering from one mountain fastness to another.

He soon came to see Jericho as insufficiently secure from his enemies. He rebuilt and re-equipped the fortress of Alexandrium, high above the Jordan Valley in central Palestine. In a bare spot, high in the mountains to the east of the Dead Sea, he rebuilt the sinister fortress-palace of Machaerus, which has still to be excavated. It was here that his son Antipas watched Salome dance and, in return, gave her the head of John the Baptist who had been imprisoned in the dungeons. Matthew 14:1-11.

To the west of the Dead Sea, on a flat-topped mountain, he built a fortress city. Initially Masada had been fortified by the Maccabees. It was a place that ideally suited Herod's paranoid nature. Around this self-sufficient, fortified city there was a sheer drop of 1,300 feet to the western shore of the Dead Sea.

To the northern extremity he built a three-tiered palace: a

villa on each of three terraces below the top level of the rock and away from the fiercest glare of the sun. On the fortified plateau were vast store-rooms, administrative buildings, at least one synagogue, at least two other palaces and a variety of other structures, together with water cisterns and store-rooms.

Following the fall of Jerusalem in AD 70 the Zealots held out in Masada for three years until Roman General Silva, using Jewish slave labour from En Gedi, constructed a vast ramp and stormed the 'impregnable fortress' — to find that everyone, with the exception of a handful of women and children, had committed suicide.

In 27 BC Herod commenced extensive building work at Samaria. He built a new city contained within walls $2\frac{1}{2}$ miles long with towers at intervals. The vast, imposing gateway, even in its ruined state, is still impressive. Herod called the new town *Sebaste*, in the Greek form — Augustus-town.

Herod's summer palace was built atop an artificially constructed hill in the barren wastes to the south of Bethlehem. Excavation work on *Herodion* carried out between 1962 and 1967 revealed a circular palace with an outer diameter of 67 yards. At the four points of the compass — north, south, east and west — there were semi-circular towers with an average diameter of 17 yards. There were the usual Herodian features, including baths; and, rather eccentrically, at the foot of the artificially constructed hill was another small palace, complete with baths.

In 4 BC, not long after ordering the murder of the innocents in nearby Bethlehem, Herod was buried here. Josephus Flavius describes it thus; 'The bier was of solid gold, studded with precious stones and had a covering of purple, embroidered with various colours: on this lay the body enveloped in a purple robe, a diadem encircling the head and surmounted by a crown of gold, the sceptre beside his right hand.' *Jewish Wars* 1, XXX, ix.

Exactly where was Herod buried? Archaeologists have done much work to uncover his tomb, thus far without success.

Herod's Jerusalem

Herod's Jerusalem contained an amphitheatre, a hippodrome, a theatre, public squares and new paved streets and colonnades that covered acres of ground. These would have been substantially the king's conception. Most of them still await the spade of the archaeologist. However, on the western edge of modern Jerusalem at the Holy Land Hotel, a brave, and probably fairly accurate, model has been built of Jerusalem in AD 66 — Herod's Jerusalem.

Hebron: An Herodian structure intact

Only at Hebron is there an Herodian building almost entirely intact. The great structure built by Herod over the traditional site of the Cave of Machpelah (containing the tombs of Abraham, Sarah, Isaac, Rebekah, Jacob and Leah) has somehow escaped the ravages of centuries of conquerors. Among the reasons for this is that it is sacred to the Muslim, Christian and Jewish religions. The Muslims have added minarets at opposite corners and one or two other appendages. Apart from that the building is substantially as Herod left it. Its great outer wall, so strangely preserved, gives us an excellent idea of how the exterior of Herod's buildings would have appeared to his contemporaries.

Acre, Antioch, Byblos

Herod's building was not restricted to Palestine. At Ptolemais (Acre) he built a gymnasium, at Sidon a theatre, at Byblos new outer walls, and at Antioch a boulevard paved with marble and shaded with cloisters. He gave funds for building projects in Greek cities, including Athens. Here archaeologists have uncovered what they believe to be the base of a statue of Herod. The inscription reads: 'To Herod, friend of Rome.'

Caesarea Philippi

Of some of the building achievements of Herod archaeologists have been able to find no trace. Contemporary historians attest that Caesar Augustus gave Panias (renamed by Herod's son, Caesarea Philippi) to Herod. Panias was situated high in the Hermon Range, near the sources of the River Jordan. Here, apparently, from gratitude to Caesar, Herod built an elaborate temple to Caesar's godhead in glistening white marble. Doubtless it was against a background of this eye-dazzling edifice that Jesus asked his disciples the question, *'Whom say ye that I am?'* and elicited from Peter the reply, *'Thou art the Christ.'* Mark 8:29. In addition to this monument to Caesar worship it is believed that, in Christ's time, there were fourteen ruined temples to the worship of Baal. Indeed, the original name of Panias had been Baalinas, Baal's city. The name Panias indicated its association with the Greek gods.

In addressing this question to his disciples it is likely that Jesus had chosen his location carefully. He was deliberately setting himself against a background of three of the world's great religions and demanding a comparison between them and himself.

Herod's Temple destroyed

Most of the building on the Jerusalem temple had been completed by 9 BC. However, all work was not completed until AD 64, just two years before the beginning of the Jewish revolt. By AD 31, the probable year of Christ's crucifixion, the temple was such a source of pride to the Jews that the disciples of Jesus wanted to impress upon him its magnificence. They were shocked by his response; ' *"Do you see all these things? ... I tell you the truth, not one stone here will be left on another; every one will be thrown down." '* Matthew 24:1, 2, NIV.

The Jewish rebellion began in AD 66. Herod's temple was used as a fortress by the rebels and hence became a focus of attack by the Romans. By August AD 70 all Jerusalem had been conquered by Titus, son of Roman Emperor Vespasian — all Jerusalem *except* the temple. The Zealots refused to surrender. Against the express instructions of Titus Roman soldiers set fire to the woodwork of the temple buildings and threw a torch into the inner sanctum itself. The fire burned furiously; even gold melted. The destruction was so complete that, literally, not one stone was left upon another. Indeed, the whole of Jerusalem was rubbled over until AD 135 when Emperor Hadrian gave orders that the rubble be levelled and that a new, Roman city be built on the site of Old Jerusalem.

Herod had made the temple (in the words of Josephus Flavius) 'as complete as he was able'. Perhaps he believed that he was ensuring the full return of God to his holy city. He did not realize that, just prior to his death, there had been born into the world a new High Priest whose teaching and sacrifice would render the sacrificial system of the temple obsolete.

Nevertheless, it was the building to which the child was taken to be circumcised whom Herod had sought to murder in his massacre of the innocents. It was the building which that child grown to manhood deemed sufficiently sacred to call his 'Father's house of prayer'. It was the temple to which Messiah would come, where he would teach and heal — but which he would replace.

Jerusalem and Jerusalem's temple enjoyed her finest hour of splendour, in one sense at least, under Herod 'the Great'. No previous king approached Herod 'the Great' in what he had done to make the city 'a glory among the nations'. But seventy-four years after his death her glory lay in the dust.

References
[1] J. A. Thompson, *The Bible and Archaeology*, third edition (1982), page 290.
[2] Ibid, pages 294, 297.
[3] Kathleen M. Kenyon, *Archaeology of the Holy Land*, fourth edition (1979), pages 240, 306.
[4] J. A. Thompson, *op cit*, page 298.
[5] Rivka Gonen, *Biblical Holy Places* (1987), page 154.
[6] W. F. Albright, *Archaeology of Palestine* (1956), page 154.

Digging up the New Testament

The city built on the site of Jerusalem following Hadrian's AD 134-135 visit was given the name *Aelia Capitolina*. The name Jerusalem was not revived.

The *Cardo Maximus* (main street) of this Roman city has been excavated. An ancient street map has been discovered. Archaeologists working in various parts of the city have found that Hadrian's builders often made use of Herodian stone. Beneath the present-day Damascus Gate, for example, has been found evidence of both Roman and Herodian gates.

Helena's Holy Places

In AD 326 Helena, mother of Constantine, visited *Aelia Capitolina*. She shared with her son, the first Christian Byzantine Emperor, an enthusiasm for Christianity. Her religion was, however, an interesting mix of confused Christianity and religions and superstitions current in pre-Christian Rome.

Helena's purpose in visiting the Holy Land — and *Aelia Capitolina* — was to find 'the true cross' and locate the sites associated with the life, death and resurrection of Jesus. This she did with suspicious precision. It speaks volumes for the power and authority of the ancient Christian church that the majority of Christian pilgrims — and archaeologists such as Father Jerome Murphy-O'Connor[1] — accept Helena's identifications as authentic. According to early Christian historian

Eusebius, Helena's identifications were informed by 'divine inspiration'.

In Bethlehem Helena selected a complex of caves as the place of Christ's birth. Above them are now situated the Church of the Nativity built by Constantine (in the fourth century) and the Church of St. Catherine built by Francis Joseph (in the nineteenth century). The only comment that archaeology can make is that in the Bethlehem of the turn of the eras dwellings were one-roomed affairs built over the caves that sheltered the animals owned by the family. Hence an 'inn' might well have been situated over a complex of caves. . . .

In Jerusalem Helena made many 'positive identifications' both within the city and on the Mount of Olives. Among her discoveries were 'the remains of the Cross in an underground cistern'[2], and a Temple to Zeus which, she asserted, had been built over the sites of Christ's death and resurrection. Her identification was more or less unchallenged until Dr. Conrad Schick, after his work on Hezekiah's tunnel, excavated the Garden Tomb north of the Damascus Gate. While biblical archaeologists like Professor W. S. McBirnie[3] adduce New Testament and archaeological data *for* the Garden Tomb and *against* Helena's site, the views of the devout who, like Murphy-O'Connor, are passionately devoted to the Church of the Holy Sepulchre, must be respected.[4]

The dispassionate archaeologist can only weigh the evidence and point out that Roman crucifixions were invariably carried out by the side of major roads for maximum visibility; and that, to contemporaries, Helena's choice was 'contrary to all expectations'.[5] It would appear that prior to Helena's visit the Temple of Zeus had not been associated with the site of the death and resurrection of Jesus by local Christians.

Centuries of Christian devotion, dogmatic identification and shrine-building have stretched the credibility of the thinking person and made the task of the archaeologist more difficult. Christian archaeologist Professor Siegfried Horn is unusual in making the following sensible comment regarding the debate between the Church of the Holy Sepulchre and the Garden Tomb: 'To know the exact place of our Saviour's crucifixion and burial is not important, and at the most it can impart only an edifying impression on the pious visitor to Jerusalem. It is much more important to know that Christ rose from the tomb, and that we are not serving a dead Saviour. The early Christians do not seem to have attached much importance to the traditional sites of Christ's ministry. They were more concerned about preaching his life, death, and resurrection.'[6]

Digging up Jerusalem

Three sites within the walls of the Old City can, with some certainty, be directly identified with places named in the gospel accounts. The Pools of Bethesda in the north-east corner of the city have been excavated. One of these was associated with a miracle performed by Jesus. The Herodian platform which now supports the Dome of the Rock and the Mosque of El Aksa, once, without question, supported the Temple of the Jews. The Citadel, near the Jaffa Gate, was built over the Herodian palace and incorporates one of its towers. This palace was, almost certainly, the scene of an episode in the trial of Jesus.

Added to these three authentic sites may well be the Lithostratos, the Roman courtyard excavated beneath the Convent of the Sisters of Zion. While fashionable debate currently favours a second-century date, significant evidence continues to support the view that this was once part of the outer courtyard of the Antonia Fortress. If this identification is correct then the large slabs rutted with grooves worn by chariot wheels once echoed to the shrieks of a mob who wanted the Roman governor to crucify an innocent, thorn-crowned Galilean.

In New Testament times two hills to the south of the present-day Old City were enclosed within the city walls. One of these, now called Mount Zion, was then known as the Upper City. The other, the Mount Ophel of the Old Testament, would then have been the oldest part of Jerusalem. One of the main streets of Old Jerusalem, leading from the Upper City, over Ophel, and down into the Kidron Valley has been, in part, excavated. This terraced roadway dates from *circa* 150 BC. It would have been a major thoroughfare of the city at the time of Jesus.

A large house has been excavated on the slopes of the Upper City and evidence has been produced to associate it with the High Priests of the first century and before. Beyond the Brook Kidron, on the lower slopes of the Mount of Olives, is the Garden of Gethsemane. The New Testament accounts leave little room for speculation regarding its location. Therefore, on the night of his arrest, Jesus would have been led by the temple guard up the Maccabean stairway, the terraced street. It would have represented the most direct route — probably the *only* route — between the Kidron Valley and the High Priest's house where Jesus faced his first trial.

The identification of the Mount of Olives, often referred to in the gospel account, has never been called into question. These days it is dotted with shrines. Nevertheless, the olive groves and limestone paths are still evocative of the New Testament, as is the old 'Palm Sunday road' from Bethany.

A great deal of archaeological excavation continues to be carried out to the south-east of the present-day Old City. Much of this is concerned with the Second Temple structures and pre-Christian Jerusalem.

After Herod the Great

As previously stated, Herod the Great would appear to have met his death in 4 BC. Augustus Caesar decided to divide the domains of Herod between his three sons. Herod Archelaus became Ethnarch of Samaria, Judaea and the northern part of Idumaea. Herod Antipas was given Galilee and Peraea. Herod Philip received a tract of territory to the north of Galilee as far as the Hermon Range.

Even before the accession of Herod Archelaus, the Jews revolted against the prospect of his rule. With just cause it was believed that his cruelty was even greater than that of his execrated father. He occurs once in the gospel account (Matthew 2:22). Here Mary and Joseph and the child Jesus, having successfully escaped from the murderous attempts of Herod the Great by taking refuge in Egypt, discovered that Archelaus had succeeded him. On the basis of that information they took their decision to return to Galilee, rather than settle in Judaea.

Resistance to the rule of Archelaus continued and, on the death of Augustus and the accession of Tiberius in AD 14, Archelaus was removed. From AD 14 the territories over which he had ruled reverted to direct Roman supervision. In total there were fourteen procurators appointed by Rome during the period of direct rule. Three of these are named in the New Testament: Pontius Pilate (AD 26-36), Antonius Felix (AD 52-60), and Porcius Festus (AD 60-62).

Archelaus was not the only one of Herod the Great's sons to figure in the gospels. Herod Philip receives a mention, and Herod Antipas is never far from the surface of the narrative. Jesus called him, 'that fox' (Luke 13:32); he was directly responsible for the arrest and decapitation of John the Baptist (Matthew 14:1-12; Mark 6:14-29; Luke 9:7-9). In addition, mid-trial, when Pilate realized that Jesus was a Galilean and that Antipas was in Jerusalem for the Passover, he sent Jesus to be tried before him (Luke 23:1-12).

The mad Emperor Caligula deposed Antipas and banished him to Gaul. His tetrarchy was given to his wife's brother —

a grandson of Herod the Great — Herod Agrippa I. Agrippa was also given a part of the territories previously directly ruled from Rome, as well as the tetrarchy of Herod Philip. Agrippa features in the book of Acts as an enemy of the infant Christian church. He executed James and imprisoned Peter (Acts 12:2-4), and when Peter escaped he ordered the execution of the guards (verses 11-19). He met his death suddenly and mysteriously in Caesarea in AD 44 (Acts 12:21-23). The contemporary Jewish historian Josephus Flavius supports the gospel account that Herod Agrippa I died an exceedingly painful death[7].

Rome considered that his son, Herod Agrippa II, 17, was too young to administer the vast territories his father had controlled. Hence direct Roman rule was extended for a time. By AD 54, at the accession of the Emperor Nero, Herod Agrippa II ruled almost all the domains his great ancestor Herod the Great had once controlled. He continued to do so until his death at the end of the first century.

The apostle Paul's first arrest was ordered by Felix who, while procurator during the period of direct rule, had married the sister of Herod Agrippa II, Drusilla (Acts 21:27-24:27). It was before Porcius Festus that Paul appealed to be tried before Caesar, the right of a Roman citizen (Acts 25:1-12). On one occasion Herod Agrippa II, accompanied by his sister Bernice, at Caesarea, heard Paul preach and made his sardonic reply, 'Do you think you're going to make *me* a Christian?' (See Acts 25:13-26:32.)

The length of the reign of Herod Agrippa II, almost half a century, means that there are many more coins dating from his period than from the reigns of his predecessors. A number of coins have been found which date from the period of the fifth procurator. Pontius Pilate, never noted for tact, even succeeded in offending the Jews by his coinage. His coins were covered with pagan symbols. No reference is made to Pilate on the coins, but they are assigned to the year of a given procurator only on the basis of dating material that refers to the emperors. Inevitably there was a time when the very existence of Pontius Pilate was doubted by the highbrow critics. Equally inevitably a stone has been found bearing the name of Pontius Pilate. It is a dedication stone from the Roman theatre at Caesarea.

New Testament accuracy confirmed

The main sites associated with the ministry of Jesus in Galilee, Judaea and the surrounding areas have been positively identified. With regard to the sites of Bethlehem, Nazareth, the Sea of Gaililee, Cana, Nain, Capernaum and Chorazin 'there can be no reasonable doubt'.[8]

Much of the Galilean ministry of Jesus centred around Capernaum. Excavations of this once thriving centre of trade stretch over one mile of the Galilean shore. First to be excavated, and partly restored, was an ancient synagogue. Built of white limestone — by contrast with the native stone, black basalt — and in the Roman style, it was for many years assumed to have been the first-century synagogue mentioned so many times in the four gospels and built at the expense of a Roman centurion (Luke 7:5).

The dating of other synagogues in the Galilee region led archaeologists to doubt the first-century date of the Capernaum synagogue. It is now assumed that in the military campaign of Vespasian and Titus in Galilee that all synagogues were systematically destroyed. However, research done between 1986 and 1987 beneath the existing ruins has provided conclusive evidence that, as might be expected, one synagogue was built over the ruins of another. Hence, while the present, visible ruins almost certainly date from the fourth century, they are those of a synagogue built over the site of the first-century synagogue presided over by Jairus and in which Jesus performed certain of his miracles.

The absence of shrines in the Galilean region has made the

work of the archaeologists considerably easier, enabling them to be more objective in their identifications. At the time of Jesus there would have been as many as twenty settlements around the shoreline of Galilee with a population of in excess of 20,000. Today there is only one. It was built between AD 14 and 22 by Herod Antipas and named after the Roman Caesar Tiberius. Antipas had it built over an ancient Jewish cemetery. For this reason it was shunned by the devout for much of the first century. Indeed, although it is mentioned in the gospels, there is no evidence that Jesus actually preached there. After the fall of Jerusalem in AD 70, however, Tiberias became the main centre for Jewish scholarship.

Among the New Testament writers Luke takes greatest pains in setting the events associated with the life of Jesus and the growth of the early church against the background of secular history. It is, perhaps for this reason that the nineteenth-century critics subjected Luke to the most intensive investigations. Destroy the credibility of Luke's writings in his gospel and the book of Acts, and the historicity of the whole of the Testament would have been undermined. F. C. Baur of the Tubingen School asserted that statements in Acts 'can only be looked upon as intentional deviations from historic truth'.[9]

Other biblical researchers and archaeologists, most notably Sir William Ramsay, began to do their own research on the historical accuracy of Luke's two books, more especially the book of Acts. Ramsay began from a position of extreme scepticism with regard to the biblical record; 'I began with a mind unfavourable to it, for the ingenuity and apparent completeness of the Tubingen theory had at one time quite convinced me.' However, after a detailed and painstaking investigation of the book of Acts and of the topography, antiquities and society of Asia Minor, Ramsay was able to make the following statement: 'It was gradually borne in upon me that in various detail the (biblical) narrative showed marvellous truth. In fact, beginning with the fixed idea that the work was essentially a second-century composition and never relying on its evidence as trustworthy for first-century conditions, I gradually came to find it a useful ally in some obscure and difficult investigations.' [10]

What redirected the thinking of Ramsay, and eventually a whole generation of Bible scholars, was the fact that archaeological investigation demonstrated that the historical, geographical, topographical, and political atmosphere of the books of Luke and Acts authenticated in the minutest detail Luke's sound, historical and political sense, as well as his grasp of geography.

The Tubingen school had, in particular, attacked Luke's accuracy in two respects: 1. His dating of the birth of Christ: *'In those days Caesar Augustus issued a decree that a census should be taken of the entire Roman world. (This was the first census that took place while Quirinius was governor of Syria.)'* (Luke 2:1, 2, NIV.) 2. His date for the emergence of John the Baptist: *'In the fifteenth year of the reign of Tiberius Caesar — when Pontius Pilate was governor of Judaea, Herod tetrarch of Galilee, his brother Philip tetrarch of Iturea and Trachonitis, and Lysanias tetrarch of Abilene — during the high priesthood of Annas and Caiaphas, the word of God came to John son of Zachariah.'* (Luke 3:1, 2, NIV.)

It had long been accepted by all Bible scholars that when the BC/AD dating system had been worked out centuries after Christ, the dating for the birth of Christ had been miscalculated by between four and six years. Hence the fact that Herod the Great reigned from 37 BC to 4 BC was a problem to neither school of biblical interpretation. However, F. C. Baur made much of the impossibility of a world-wide census and that the governorship of Syria by Quirinius overlapped with the reign of Herod the Great.

After years of research Ramsay was able to explain the apparent difficulties very clearly. He pointed out that Luke had used the present tense of the verb deliberately and had meant 'that Augustus had ordered enrolments to be regularly taken', that is, that he had laid down the principle of systematic 'enrolment' in the Roman world, not made arrangements for taking one single, world-wide census. He produced detailed records of these repeated 'enrolments' in Egypt. Further, he provided evidence that the enrolments were, generally, separated by fourteen years. He even discovered that the census which necessitated the journey of Mary and Joseph from Nazareth to Bethlehem was probably two years late. The extraordinary circumstances in Palestine and Syria, Ramsay argued, accounted for the delay of the census in Herod's kingdom. [11]

Similarly Ramsay had an ingenious way of dealing with Baur's assertion that Quirinius was *not* governor of Syria in the year of Christ's birth, 4 BC, but that his governorship commenced some years later. Ramsay found that the Greek word translated 'governor' in Luke 2:2 merely implied 'oversight'. He produced inscriptions that proved that Quirinius had had 'oversight' over Syria during two separate periods. Professor F. F. Bruce, half a century on, examined Ramsay's evidence. He succeeded in producing more artefacts to substantiate the view that Quirinius was, in fact, the imperial legate in Syria during the final years of the reign of Herod the Great. [12]

The Tubingen attack on the accuracy of Acts ridiculed the idea that *'a severe famine' 'spread over the entire Roman world . . . during the reign of Claudius'* (Acts 11:27, 28, NIV). Ramsay discovered in the writings of Roman historian Suetonius many references to famine prices under Claudius Caesar. In the writings of Dio Cassius and Tacitus he found references to two famines in Rome, as well as famines elsewhere in the

Mediterranean world. Ramsay discovered in *Eusebius* references to a famine in Greece. He discovered an inscription in Asia Minor to a widespread famine in the Roman provinces there during the reign of Claudius. Indeed he found that the imperial reign of Claudius (AD 41-54) was marked by a succession of bad harvests which caused serious famines. He linked one such famine with the collection made by Paul on behalf of the Jerusalem church in AD 46.

During Paul's first missionary journey he visited Cyprus. In the course of thirty-five years Cyprus had had four different types of Roman government. Displaying acute political awareness, Luke was careful to give the correct title of 'deputy' to a Roman official mentioned in Acts 13:7. This displayed his awareness of the nature of the Roman government in the exact year of Paul's visit. The 'deputy's' name was Sergius Paulus. Among Ramsay's discoveries on Cyprus was an inscription bearing the name of this deputy.

The Asia Minor of Paul's missionary journeys was a jigsaw of provincial frontiers. Ramsay demonstrated that Luke was meticulous in his account, both with regard to geographical and political frontiers. On certain points of detail Luke's accuracy had been challenged; the archaeological discoveries of Ramsay and his successors have proved Luke, not his nineteenth- and twentieth-century detractors, to be correct. From Luke's description in Acts 16:12, 13 of where the gospel was first preached in Europe — at Philippi — French archaeologists working in Philippi between 1914 and 1938 were able to pinpoint the exact spot where the preaching occurred. They also excavated the 'market place' to which Paul and Silas were dragged in the course of the narrative. Similarly archaeological discoveries in Athens have authenticated the detail of Luke's account. Two Greek writers, Pausanias and Philostratus, were, like Paul, impressed by the number of religious images as well as the altar with an inscription, *'To the Unknown God'*.

232

Ramsay concluded his exhaustive examination of the historical data of the book of Acts with these words:

'Luke is a historian of the first rank; not merely are his statements of fact trustworthy; he is possessed of the true historic sense; he fixes his mind on the idea and plan that rules in the evolution of history, and proportions the scale of his treatment to the importance of each incident. He seizes the important and critical events and shows that true nature at greater length, while he touches lightly, or omits entirely, much that was valueless for his purpose. In short, this author should be placed along with the very greatest of the historians.'[13]

Not for the first time, the Book was right — and the critics were wrong.

References
[1] Jerome Murphy-O'Connor, *The Holy Land* (second edition 1986).
[2] Rivka Gonen, *Biblical Holy Places* (1987), page 131.
[3] *The Search for the Tomb of Jesus* (1978).
[4] Anyone interested in the debate about the Garden Tomb and the Church of the Holy Sepulchre as sites for the crucifixion and resurrection of Jesus should read Bill White, *A Special Place: A Wide-Angle View of the Garden Tomb* (1990).
[5] Eusebius (AD 336), *Life of the Empress Helena*, chapter 3, pages 28-30.
[6] Siegfried H. Horn, *The Spade Confirms the Book* (1980), pages 181, 182.
[7] Josephus Flavius, *Antiquities of the Jews*, XIX, viii, 2.
[8] G. E. Wright and F. V. Wilson, *Westminster Historical Atlas* (1958), cited J. A. Thompson, *The Bible and Archaeology* (third edition 1982), page 371.
[9] Cited J. A. Thompson, *op cit*, page 385.
[10] W. M. Ramsay, *St. Paul the Traveller* (1897), pages 7 *et seq.*
[11] Ibid, pages 4-17, 174-179.
[12] F. F. Bruce, *Are the New Testament Documents Reliable?* (1946), page 85; J. A. Thompson, *op cit*, pages 385-388.
[13] W. M. Ramsay, *The Bearing of Recent Discovery on the Trustworthiness of the New Testament* (1915), page 222.

IN
CONCLUSION

The message of the Book

Taste and see . . .

The Bible is not true because the findings of archaeologists authenticate as fact the details of its narrative. Or because, against the longest odds imaginable, the discovery of ancient manuscripts in the last 150 years or so has demonstrated that its text has not been corrupted by time. Or because, down the centuries, men have been prepared to be burned for translating it, or imprisoned for reading it, or to face forced labour camps for distributing it.

The artefacts of archaeology and the manuscripts of history are merely evidences for faith.

Light *is* light. Darkness *is* darkness. They are not what they are because of chemical tests.

Truth *is* truth.

And so the Bible is self-authenticating. The Bible is the sort of book that a man could not write if he would, and would not write if he could. The content of the Book is such that men or women, by exposing themselves to it, can discover that it is inspired by God.

The challenge is: Taste! See! Read! Discover! Adventure! And it will not be long before you find you are adventuring with God.

The Bible *is* far more than 'the world's best-seller'; *has* more, far more than 'the *ring* of truth'.

Its readers find it to be as real as the blood pulsing through their arteries, as real as the earth beneath their feet. The adventure with God into which it leads brings the reader —

✻ *to his roots.* Matter plus Time plus Chance do *not* make a world. Man, matter and time exist by divine fiat. Man was made in the image of an all-powerful, all-knowing, all-loving Creator God. His roots are among eternal things.

✻ *to purposeful living.* The God who made man in his image loves him as an everlasting Father. Life *is* more than a dusty scuffle over a parched terrain between Point Birth and Point Death. Life *is* more than a catalogue of accidents. Life *is* more than a nightmare between two eternities. Life committed to God has purpose and aim, and both are tied up in a relationship of trust into which all comers are invited.

✻ *to ultimate security.* God's love is stronger than that of any parent. The God of the Bible gives no copper-bottomed guarantee that his children will not encounter problems and difficulties. What he *does* guarantee is that when the problems and difficulties come, he will walk by their side. That he hurts when they hurt. That no hurt will come their way until it has been sieved through his love, grace and power. And that, even when it strikes, it will be made to work for the ultimate good of the sufferer.

✻ *to fear-free living.* God is Sovereign, all-powerful. The world is more like a ship than an iceberg. The iceberg cracks off from the polar ice-cap in a thunderous explosion, after that its course and destiny are subject to all kinds of uncertainties. A ship has a captain, a navigator, charts, maps, and the whole business of navigational equipment. The God of the Bible is a Captain who says, 'Trust me regardless of the storms and I'll guide the vessel into an eternal harbour. Examine my record as set out in the Book. Look at the events foretold years before they happened and how they came to pass. See how I have set out my scenario of the future. Trust me in the little things of Time; I am concerned with the details of your life. Trust me in the big things of Eternity; I want to guide you through the worst to the ultimate best.'

�帯 *to guilt-free living.* Neither the Bible nor the God revealed in its pages have any illusions about man. God made men and women perfect. On behalf of the rest of us, the first Adam gave in to the force of evil present on the planet. That force led man, with his consent, into depravity and corruption. The natural tendency of the human choice-mechanism is towards the worst, rather than the best. But the Bible tells how, though eternal right must be maintained, eternal love found a way to save sinners through the second Adam, God's own Son. That God gives both sin-sorrow and forgiveness; both the impulse to desire the best (against man's own nature), and the new life that *is* the best (against man's own deserts).

✝ *to ultimate hope.* The Bible promises that a glorious new world — beyond the pain and injustice of the present — awaits those who enter the new life amid the sorrows and uncertainties of the now. This is its message. In an uncertain world the assurance of eternity is possible. In an evil-choked world, forgiveness, acceptance and high-level living are possible. In a world of conflict it is possible to live with supernatural peace. In a world of heartbreak it is possible to have a joy of the sort that it is in no man's power to take from you.

It's all subject to choice. Man's choice.

God has opened up the way through his Son, the second Adam. *Everything* is possible through trusting him, and establishing a day-by-day relationship with him. *That* is the message of the Bible.

All sounds too good to be true?

There's only one way to find out.

Taste and see.

Take the Book down from the shelf. Risk exposing yourself to its influence, to the story and magnetism of the God revealed in its pages — and to the Man in the Book who, even now, is promising you a new life.

Why was the Bible written?

Before we read a book we may want to know something about the author's reason for writing it.

What is he trying to say? Is he the right person to say it? Does what he says have meaning for the contemporary world?

By now we know that the Bible was written by many different authors over a long period of time. We have been at pains to prove that behind the various authors is a single divine Author with a single unifying theme. We have demonstrated the miraculous ways in which that single Author safeguarded his Book from corruption over the centuries and, right on time, permitted evidence to come to light to lend substance to faith.

But what about that purpose or 'unifying theme'?

Paul sets it out crisply in a letter to Timothy: *'From infancy you have known the holy scriptures, which are able to make you wise for salvation through faith in Christ Jesus. All Scripture is God-breathed and is useful for teaching, rebuking, correcting and training in righteousness, so that the man of God may be thoroughly equipped for every good work.'* 2 Timothy 3:15-17, NIV.

There we have it. Origin of Book: *'God-breathed.'* Object of Book: *'useful' for human beings*.

First of all we had better examine what is meant by the expression *'God-breathed'.* What *did* God have to do with the Bible?

Then we will examine the ways Paul says it can be *'useful'.*

1. *What did God have to do with it?* Just before Paul told Timothy that the Bible was 'God-breathed' he had been talking about conditions in 'the last days'. For Paul 'the last days' were both present and future. For us 'the last days' are just present. 'In the last days', Paul told Timothy, people would enthrone themselves, and dethrone God. This enthroning of

self and dethroning of God would lead to a misdirection of life — and fearful consequences would ensue. People would become boastful, proud, abusive, rebellious against all authority, without love or natural affection, lovers of money, ungrateful, disobedient to parents, unholy and unforgiving. Their religion, he said, would be characterized by 'a form of godliness' while 'denying its power'. Their religion would be one of externals and forms; but the power, the miraculous element, they would deny. Paul went on to tell Timothy that a special breed of preacher would arise, prepared to humour their hearers by reverencing externals, while denying the Power which gave point to it all.

Timothy was a preacher. Paul didn't want him to be *that* kind of preacher. So, having defined the prevailing mood, he started to talk about the Bible. Scripture, he said, was breathed out of the mouth of God. What was breathed out of the mouth of God, the many and various writers wrote or spoke. In other words, God did not dictate the Bible. He inspired the minds of its authors, leaving them to express his inspiration in their own words and thought forms.

Right off we have one reason why the Bible was written: *It was God speaking his mind.* The Bible was a miraculous means, devised by a God of miracles, in order to communicate his mind, his purposes and himself to the children made in his image. The Bible is the Word of God through the words of men. God did not ask human authors to take dictation. He allowed the human authors to express themselves in terms appropriate to their culture. He permitted them to develop their own syntax, vocabulary and literary style. God was speaking through men, and men were speaking from God. The Bible has a double authorship. This is what is implied by 'God-breathed'.

2. *The Bible's usefulness.* Paul linked three words with the Bible's usefulness: 'salvation', 'Christ', and 'faith'.

So the first purpose of the Bible, Paul tells Timothy, is to instruct his readers about *salvation*. And salvation is a very big word. Much is implied in it. Salvation begins when a man senses his need; as long as he thinks he can manage on his own there will be no salvation. When he senses his sinfulness he will reach out to a Power outside of himself. That 'reaching out' will be 'sin-sorrow' or repentance.

Even before the fall of the first Adam, and the entry of sin into the world, God had a contingency plan to meet the emergency. God's whole universe was built on law. Law said sin must be punished by death. And law was an expression of the character of God, the gracious One.

In both Old and New Testaments law is underlined. Through the words of both the prophets of the Old Testament and the apostles of the New the penalty of lawlessness, law-breaking, sin — was death.

God's central purpose in the Old Testament was to fore-shadow the contingency plan to be put into practice to deal with the sin problem. It was the message of the sacrificial system in tabernacle and temple. It was the essence of the prophets' messages. It was the point of their prophecies.

Sin was condemned. Sin's penalty outlined. Sin's solution prefigured, foreshadowed in a hundred different ways.

And the solution to the sin problem was in the second word Paul emphasized to Timothy: '*Christ*'. Every page of the Old Testament rustles with the rumour of a Coming One. One who would be, at the same time, 'the mighty God' and 'the suffering servant'. One who, like the lambs offered on the altar, would be 'without blemish', 'holy, harmless, undefiled'. As the penitent confessed his sins over the head of the innocent lamb to be slaughtered, so God would send his own Lamb. The 'Lamb of God' — in all things perfect, without blemish — would die for the sins of a fallen race. The sin problem would be resolved in the death of God's son. Isaiah (7:14) said he would be born of a virgin. Psalm 132:11 said he would be of the house of David. Micah (5:2) said he would be born in Bethlehem. Genesis (49:10) said he would be of the tribe of Judah. Isaiah (53:3) said that he would be rejected by his own people. Psalm 118:22, 23 said that this rejection would involve the rulers. Zechariah (11:12, 13) said that he would be sold for thirty pieces of silver and that the money would be given to a potter. Zechariah further said that his side would be pierced (12:10), and that his disciples would forsake him (13:7). Isaiah's fifty-third chapter had most to say about the coming one: he would suffer what man deserved to suffer; he would be silent before his accusers; he would be buried in a rich man's tomb; he would be crucified with thieves; he would pray for his persecutors. . . . The Psalmist (16:10) knew that he would rise from the dead.

These detailed predictions, made centuries before the birth of Jesus Christ, were fulfilled in his life, death and resurrection. The gospels portray him as 'the Son of God' who, 'at the foundation of the world', had been one with the Father in love for the human race, and that the plan for the redemption of the fallen race had been entered by them both willingly.

The gospel writers presented Christ as the perfect sacrifice for sin. Paul in his letters explained the theology of it all. Christ was the Representative or Substitute for sinful man when he died on the cross on Calvary. By identification with the dying Saviour, the sins of the penitent would die. Through the Saviour's burial was symbolized the burial of sin, lost for ever in the fathomless depths of the Father's forgetfulness. In the resurrection was symbolized the accession of the sinner to a new life through a new birth.

The New Testament's revelation of Christ reaches its climax in the last of the sixty-six books of the Bible. In the Book of Revelation is represented in symbol the whole plan of salvation from the Fall of the first Adam, through the redemption brought about by the second Adam (Jesus), to the final restoration of all things when God's eternal kingdom will be set up at the Second Coming of Jesus.

Revelation presents a vivid picture of Jesus returning in his glory, his holy angels with him. Those who would rise from the grave to meet him, all the living who would ascend from the earth to meet him, would be those depending solely on the merits of the Lamb of God. In vision John (who wrote Revelation) saw a numberless multitude *'from every nation, tribe, people and language' 'standing before the throne and in front of the Lamb . . . wearing white robes'* and singing, ' *"Salvation belongs to our God, who sits on the throne, and to the Lamb."* ' Revelation 7:9, 10, NIV.

The third word used by Paul to explain why the Bible was *'useful'* for human beings was *faith.*

Elsewhere Paul explained that the Scriptures were *'able to make you wise for salvation through faith in Christ Jesus'.* In short: The central purpose of the Bible is to bring us to Christ who, in turn, is the bringer of salvation. But the object of the Scriptures in pointing us to Christ is not simply to provide us with information about him to enable us to understand and admire him. 'Scripture bears witness to Christ, not in order to satisfy our curiosity but in order to draw from us a response of faith.'[1]

Faith and *trust* are synonyms in the New Testament. The object of Scripture is to represent Jesus as absolutely worthy of our trust, to give us every reason to place implicit faith in him and in his sacrifice for sin.

Faith/trust was the key to it all. ' *"The righteous will live by faith,"* ' insisted Paul (Galatians 3:11, NIV). *'It is by grace you have been saved, through faith — and this not from yourselves, it is the gift of God — not by works, so that no one can boast.'* Ephesians 2:7-9, NIV.

And how was this all-important gift of faith received by

the believer? *'Faith comes from hearing the message, and the message is heard through the word of Christ.'* Romans 10:17, NIV.

The central purpose of Scripture: to testify to Jesus Christ in order to evoke faith in him, in order to bring salvation to the believer.

Jesus Christ is the central figure in Scripture. The Old Testament foreshadows him from its opening to its concluding chapters. The New Testament gospels describe his life, ministry, death and resurrection. And, in case anyone could have missed the point, the letters of Paul, John, Peter and James, together with John's book of Revelation, make the significance of the life, death and resurrection of Jesus for the sinner crystal clear. The letter to the Romans, in particular, represents a distillation of New Testament theology.

Through the death and resurrection of Christ the sinner was 1. JUSTIFIED: the guilt of sin was removed and the merits of Jesus covered the sinner; 2. SANCTIFIED: a longer process, this; the work of a life-time. As the sinner matured in his relationship with Jesus Christ, the power of sin waned in his experience; 3. GLORIFIED: the actual presence of sin, the last vestiges of it, would be removed at the return of Jesus Christ.

To the Christian the central purpose of Scripture could be summarized in the words employed by the apostle John to describe the aim of his gospel: *'That you may believe that Jesus is the Christ, the Son of God, and that by believing you may have life in his name.'* John 20:31, NIV.

References
[1] John Stott, *Understanding the Bible* (revised edition, 1984), page 22.

24

The Man in the Book

Jesus Christ is the central figure of the Bible.

The same nineteenth-century German scholars who dated the New Testament books in the second century or later (and have been proved so conclusively wrong) dismissed Jesus as no more than an inspirational preacher. Some even doubted that he had existed at all. In the early twentieth century Rudolf Bultmann of Marburg University contended that the Bible was so full of myth and legend that 'we can know almost nothing concerning the life and personality of Jesus'.

Meanwhile archaeological finds have authenticated the details of the biblical account to a remarkable degree. The context of personalities, boundaries and political systems in which New Testament events occurred can no longer be doubted.

Oxford University's E. P. Thompson in *Jesus and Judaism* (1985) has affirmed: 'The dominant view today seems to be that we can know pretty well what Jesus was out to accomplish, that we can know a lot about what he said, and that these two things make sense within the world of first century Judaism.'

Jesus in history

The nineteenth century sceptics who doubted the existence of Jesus and the dating of the rise of Christianity had their views shaken by the discovery of a considerable number of references to Christ and Christianity in the works of Roman historians and in contemporary documents.

In 1889 Dr. Rendel Harris found at St. Catherine's on Sinai a Syriac translation of a defence of Christianity addressed to the

243

Emperor Antonius Pius by an Athenian philosopher in AD 140. It shed a great deal of light on the early history and beliefs of Christianity.

Study of Roman documents proved enlightening. Between the Resurrection and the conversion of Constantine no Roman emperor was free from anxiety about the 'Christian question'.

In AD 108 Gaius Plinius Secundus ('the Younger Pliny'), Governor of the province of Bithynia in Asia Minor, wrote to Emperor Trajan about his problems. There was religious unrest. Temples were practically deserted and, in some cases, the services discontinued. There was a recession in agriculture because people were no longer buying beasts for sacrifice on the same scale as before. The fault lay with some people called 'Christians' whose loyalty was highly suspect because they refused to offer sacrifices to the god-emperor. He had brought many Christians to trial but had failed to find evidence of criminal activity. All he had been able to accuse them of was 'degraded and extravagant superstition'. They met on a certain day each week to sing hymns to Christ 'as to a god' and to bind themselves on solemn oath to keep the moral law: not to rob or steal, or commit adultery, or defraud. The service was followed by a ritual meal together. Everything was harmless on the surface, but their attitude towards the Emperor, asserted Pliny, made them highly suspect. Pliny, *Correspondence with Trajan*, letters 96 and 97.

In AD 112 Cornelius Tacitus was writing a *History of the Rome of the Emperors*. In the imperial reign of Nero there had, he said, been a great fire that had devastated Rome. To take attention from the half-mad Emperor — believed by many to have been the arsonist — the Roman authorities had picked on the Christians as scapegoats. The 'Christians', Tacitus explained for the benefit of his readers, were almost universally unpopular in Rome and suspected of all manner of doubtful, clandestine religious rites. A vast number of Christians had been arrested; the excruciating tortures to which they had been subjected and the grisly deaths they had died swung Roman opinion round in their favour.

Tacitus made it clear that *he* did not believe the Christians to have been the true incendiaries. However, their founder had been a criminal who had been executed by Pontius Pilate, procurator of Judaea, some thirty years earlier.

The death of the ringleader, averred Tacitus, had not stopped the 'pestilent superstition', but had given impetus to its growth. Now its adherents were an 'immense multitude'. Tacitus, *Annals*, XV 44.

Referring to Tacitus, Professor C. H. Dodd has said, 'Here at last, from a reputable Roman historian, we have an account of the beginnings of Christianity in the late twenties or early thirties of the first century.'[1]

Both Pliny and Tacitus, sources hostile to Christianity, provide independent corroboration of its early growth and development. So, ironically, does the Jewish *Talmud*[2]. In the era of division and dissention in the first half of the first century, says the *Talmud*, 'they hanged Jesus of Nazareth on the Eve of Passover'. He had been, apparently, 'leading Israel astray'.

There are other contemporary or near contemporary sources which provide more corroborative evidence of the existence of Jesus and (indirectly) the impact of his Resurrection felt in the wild-fire growth of the Christian Church. Among them, Josephus Flavius (a Jewish historian who was a contemporary of Jesus and his disciples), Lucian of Samosata (a second-century satirist), Suetonius (an early second-century Roman historian), as well as the writings of the Church Fathers, including Polycarp, Eusebius, Irenaeus, Ignatius, Justin, Origen, Tertullian and others. F. F. Bruce has brought together all the ancient documents and published them in his *Jesus and Christian Origins outside the New Testament*.

In the fifteenth edition of *Encyclopaedia Britannica*, volume

3, page 145, after a summary of the references to Christ in primary source material outside the New Testament, the authors conclude:

'These independent accounts prove that in ancient times even the opponents of Christianity never doubted the historicity of Jesus, which was disputed for the first time and on inadequate grounds by several authors at the end of the eighteenth, during the nineteenth and at the beginning of the twentieth centuries.'

The Jesus of the Gospels

Of course, the main source of information about Jesus is in the four gospels. They were, as we have endeavoured to demonstrate, written by men who knew Jesus personally. Hence, to the objective researcher, they are the most obvious source of information about him.

Like the rest of Scripture the gospels are self-authenticating. A good place to start reading the Bible is with the gospel of Mark. Mark was the amanuensis of Peter. How fascinating to find that it is Mark's gospel that sets Peter in the worst light! Mark's candour is most disarming. Developments we might consider important are given scant treatment. Events are described in detail which no writer could possibly have invented.

There are many details in the four gospel accounts that would have been excluded from a secular, contemporary biography. John the Baptist, at one point, is described as having his doubts regarding the authenticity of Jesus. He sent a message; *'Are you the one who was to come, or should we expect someone else?'* Like a good reporter the apostle John records the negative audience-reaction to the sermon recorded in John 6 (verses 41, 42, 43, 52, 60, 61). Jesus' loss of a mass following is candidly reported (John 6:66). Matthew records that in his home town Jesus did not work many miracles

(Matthew 13:58). Luke is prepared to report the words of unbelievers who regarded Christianity as a superstition (Acts 25:18, 19).

In an earlier chapter we have already, through the reported reactions of the apostles to the Resurrection, demonstrated that they were prepared to sacrifice effect for truth.

Short of embellishing the reputation of Jesus, again and again the gospel writers provide us with examples that accurate reportage was more important to them than making a good impression. Jesus spoke about moving mountains by faith (Matthew 21:21). He told a conscientious believer to let the dead bury their dead (Luke 9:60).

In his letters Paul showed the same disinclination to embellish his reputation. In the first chapter of his letter to the Galatians he confessed to having been a blasphemer and a persecutor and to having been turned around purely and simply by a power outside himself. The autobiographical details he provides in the letter to the Philippians chapter 3 verses 4 to 10 are far from flattering. Not without humour, he sets out the ridiculous arrogance of his former days and confesses that the religion he had espoused with such passion had been valueless; that his whole life had been valueless — apart from the resurrection power of Jesus.

The gospel writers set out bluntly the claims of Jesus to be the Christ, the Messiah, God's Son. Jesus is the only man who ever lived who claimed to be God yet was judged sane by his wisest contemporaries. Confucius did not claim to be God, nor Zoroaster, nor Buddha, nor Muhammad. They had too much sense for that, too much regard for their credibility. C. S. Lewis was correct with regard to the claims of Jesus. He said that, given such claims, Jesus had to be mad or bad — or God. No one, apparently, is suggesting that he was mad or bad. True enough, some have made the claim that he was 'Simply a great teacher'. But how could he have been —

making such claims? He did not leave us that option. He was mad, or bad or . . .

Christ in both Old and New Testaments

We have already looked at the Old Testament prophecies that foretold the coming of Jesus.

But there is more of Jesus in the Old Testament than prophecies of his coming.

Christ is the one who makes the unity between the two testaments. All sixty-six books enshrine him. The chief characters, institutions, and histories, prefigure him.

The Cross was the Tree of Life in the midst of the desolations of earth; it had been prefigured in Eden. In John's gospel it is clear that Christ saw in himself the fulfilment of Jacob's ladder, of the manna that fed Israel in the wilderness, of the rock that was smitten to provide water, of the Pillar of Fire that went before the people, of the uplifted serpent that brought healing.

In Eden, Adam, the head of the race, the image of God, fell asleep so that a bride could be taken from his side. On the cross, Jesus, the second Adam, slept the sleep of death; and, in that sleep, a spear opened his side to bring forth his Bride, the Church. (Throughout the New Testament the Church is symbolized as a bride.)

And Adam is by no means the only Old Testament character to prefigure Christ. There is Joseph, his father's most beloved son, betrayed by his brethren for pieces of silver. There is Moses the lawgiver, the deliverer, who left a palace to redeem his people; who was willing to be blotted out for the sins of his people. There is Joshua leading his people into the Promised Land. There is Boaz, Ruth's kinsman-redeemer, giving her rest and fruitfulness. There is David the warrior who never lost a battle when leading God's people and whose name means 'Beloved', who was born in Bethlehem, who as a young man overcame the giant of evil.

From first to last in Scripture it is difficult to escape its central figure: Jesus Christ. Three hundred and thirty-two distinct Old Testament prophecies were literally fulfilled in the person of Jesus. The mathematical probability of all those prophecies being fulfilled in one person is one over eighty-four with ninety-seven zeros.

His teaching

No single person has so changed the course of history, has been so loved and so despised, so hated and so adored, has so turned the bad into the good, the ugly into the beautiful — as Jesus of Nazareth.

Everywhere he went people murmured, 'What sort of man is this? Who is this?' The more we look at the person of Jesus the more we find it impossible to link him with all the other religious leaders who have emerged in the course of history. There is something about him which speaks again and again of his uniqueness. Astronaut Jim Erwin scribbled these words on the photograph that showed him walking on the moon: 'God walking on the earth, more important than Jim walking on the moon.'

And that is what we find in the gospels; God walking upon the earth. A Christ who is perfect God and perfect man, wholly God and wholly man.

His miracles astonished those who saw them. And when we read the accounts of those miracles with an open mind it becomes impossible to disbelieve in the miraculous.

But the people who *heard* Jesus also caught their breath. He spoke with astonishing authority. When he tackled the great questions of life and death and God and man he spoke with final, unquestionable authority. And yet he was manifestly humble, meek, and lowly of heart.

He worked with the same authority with which he spoke.

Sickness disappeared in his presence. Leprosy faded away. Demons shrieked and scrambled. Death gave up its claimed victims. One posse of soldiers, sent to arrest him, forgot the purpose of their mission, returning to their Temple bosses with the doubtless exasperating words, *'No man ever spoke like this man.'* A mob in Nazareth intent on pushing him over a precipice fell back at his commanding presence and piercing glare. The very Temple Guard sent to arrest him in Gethsemane at first fell back in confusion; even *there*, even *then*, he was in command of the situation.

He gathered around him the most extraordinary bunch of people. Among them were uneducated fishermen, patriotic freedom fighters, an ex-traitor, a traitor-to-be; men who were impulsive, weak, pessimistic, jealous, in all senses fallible. He saw potential in them that was only fully realized after his death and resurrection. But even in his life-time there were minor miracles in their relationships. If Simon the Zealot had met Matthew the tax collector anywhere but in the presence of Jesus he would have cut his throat. Men normally full of hate could learn to love in the presence of Jesus.

The breathtaking thing about Jesus is not just his miracles or his preaching: but his sheer character. He was anything but a typical guru, the kind of professional holy man, all pious and ascetic, we are familiar with these days. In fact he was so ordinary, so much like anyone else, that the establishment figures of his day were offended when he flouted some of their religious customs and laws. Some said, 'We can't accept *him* as Messiah. Isn't he the carpenter's son? Not only that, he mixes with sinners and ordinary folk. He never turns *anyone* away.' If we knew nothing about Jesus except what was said of him by his opponents, he would still appear as the most lovable of beings ever to walk the surface of this planet.

To everyone he showed love, there were no exceptions. The lonely, the despised, the outcast, the prostitute, the thief, the leper: he loved everybody. He gave respect and dignity to women who were despised and misused. More than anyone else in history he established the principle of the sanctity of human life. After Jesus, women and children could never again be treated as they had been previously.

His teaching was direct, sometimes unnervingly so. He unerringly exposed the selfish, greedy, proud, hypocritical, ambitious men for what they really were — and are. He pointed them to an entirely new way of living. Upset their value systems. He began with the Sermon on the Mount; 'Blessed are the poor in spirit . . . ; blessed are the meek . . .'. But the world of his day, like ours, said: Look after Number One! Act confident! Stick up for your rights! Get your own back! Don't get involved! Keep out of trouble! Who cares anyway?

By contrast the message of Jesus was: Admit your need of God. Confess your sin-sorrow. Surrender your life to God! He is either Lord *of* all, or he's not Lord *at* all! Seek first his kingdom, his righteousness! You're hurting? Forgive those who have hurt you! Make peace on earth! Trust God in every situation!

And, with the perspective of history, who can say that Jesus was wrong? His teaching meets the deepest cries and needs of men and women of all cultures, of all ages. He is the light in our darkness; the purpose in an otherwise purposeless life; the meaning in an otherwise meaningless existence.

One teaching we should never lose sight of. It is an affirmation which occurs, on average, once in every twenty-five verses in the New Testament. Jesus made a categorical promise to return to earth at the close of the age, not as a carpenter, but as King of kings.

The Cross

Christ is the central figure in Scripture.

The cross is its central symbol. All Scripture, and (according to Scripture) all history, lies beneath its shadow.

The very shape of the cross suggests the length, breadth and height of the love of God. It points to heaven from where Jesus came. It is rooted in the earth he came to redeem. The outstretched hands on the transverse beam are an invitation to all men — even to his crucifiers. Men may reject an angry God. But how can they reject a God who, even at the point of their rejection, leans forward in entreaty?

The last week before his crucifixion is the great emphasis of all four gospels. Only one day in every 350 in the life of Jesus is even referred to in the accounts of Matthew, Mark, Luke and John. But the record of the events of the last seven days takes up one third of the gospel account.

Why? Because here at the cross was the clearest depiction of the heart and mind of God. The cross tells us about man and about God, about good and about evil, about earth and about heaven. It tells us about holiness and law and righteousness and forgiveness and mercy and peace and love. It interprets the past, the present and the future.

In the mystery of the cross all other mysteries are made plain. The cross could be the darkest spot in the history of existence; but when we see it as a revelation of God it becomes the searchlight by which we can penetrate the thickest gloom and the darkest tragedy. The main beam lighting the way to eternity.

Here's the reason why God can forgive sin. Here's the reason why his law must be viewed as eternal. Here is viewed the infinite depths of evil. And here the scale of heaven's righteousness and the breadth of heaven's mercy. Here alone: the motivation to faith, hope and love. Here is the difference between Christianity and other religions and philosophies. Only Christianity can evoke faith, hope and love. Only these motivations can change a soiled and sorry life. Only the cross can do it. It's not enough to *know* what's right. What men need is not just information as to what they should do. It's the motivation to do it.

And on the Black Friday of the cross what would there have been to be seen?

The Prisoner with a crown made of the long-thorned briar crushed savagely down on his brow.

A lacerated back; the flagellum was a whip tipped with nails and bits of bone, and had been wielded by soldiers with arms like shot-putters.

The hideous shape of the cross upon the ground. Huge Roman nails, square in section, hammered through the wrists and feet of the Prisoner.

The entire hideous instrument of torture and execution, with the Prisoner upon it — *this* Prisoner, this King of Truth not of this world — hoisted in the air and savagely jolted down into the place prepared.

The cries. The intense, insupportable agony caused by the incomplete severing of the median nerves by the nails through the wrists, vibrating through the arm to explode in the brain at every movement . . . endlessly twisting, seeking relief from this onslaught on the senses . . . .

And, at length, the loud voice of a strong man crying, '*It is finished.*'

It was 3pm on the day of the Passover. On that day for fifteen centuries, and at that hour, Israel had slain her Passover lamb. Jesus died at Passover time: at the very month, day and hour of the Passover lamb. Long ago the Passover lamb had saved the firstborn of Israel. Now the firstborn of heaven became the Passover Lamb through whom the world could find its redemption.

And here is the point and purpose of Scripture.

Through the cross of Christ God is saying to men: That is where you ought to be. Jesus, my Son, hangs there in your stead. His tragedy is the tragedy of your life. You are the rebel

who should be hanged on the gallows. But stay; here is your
ladder up to heaven. This is the place of your salvation. Here
begins your lasting joy. You must meet me there at the cross
by identifying with the One on the cross. It is by this identification that I, God, can meet you in him, saying to you as
I say to him: 'My beloved son.'

His brow thorn-crushed for the wrong thoughts your mind
has harboured. His hands nail-pierced for the wrong things
your hands have done. His feet spiked through for the wandering paths your feet have trod. His back raw, laid open because
of the idolatrous gods that you have borne. His heart broken
because of the wrong things your heart has loved. His side
spear-riven to prove once and for all that the way to God's
heart is wide open.

We were there, our upturned faces contorted with hate and
scorn, our characters warped by sin. *We* swung the hammer.
We drove the nails. *We* were the crucifiers. His words, *'Father
forgive them'*, were for our hearing, and our acceptance.

Acceptance by faith. The faith that comes through hearing,
and the hearing that comes through the Word of God.

Salvation Hill. Eternity's Gate. Here our burden of guilt
can roll from our backs, unrecoverably lost. Here begins our
lasting joy, our peace that passes all understanding. Our assurance of heaven.

*'God made him who had no sin to be sin for us, so that in
him we might become the righteousness of God.'* 2 Corinthians
5:21, NIV.

The universe was built on law.

Perched on this planet-in-rebellion, we break that law a thousand times a day. And law-breaking is sin.

In God's divine, sublime reckoning his Son had died the
death that we deserve, that we might live the life that he
deserves. Our sins were nailed to that cross.

'It is finished,' he cried. Through faith the finished redemp-

tion can be ours. Through faith we can share in his resurrection; with him rise to new life, to glad, confident morning. That is the point and purpose of the whole Bible.

He is why men have been prepared to be gaoled for reading it, burned for translating it, persecuted for spreading its teachings. In it is the power that consolidates heaven, shakes hell, comforts earth, delights the Father, glorifies the Son, brings down the Spirit — and transforms the sinner.

References
[1] C. H. Dodd, *The Founder of Christianity* (1970), page 17.
[2] Babylonian *Talmud*. Tractate *Sanhedrin*, 436.